Beverly J. Irby • Genevieve Brown

The
Career
Advancement
Portfolio

CORWIN PRESS, INC.
A Sage Publications Company
Thousand Oaks, California

Copyright © 2000 by Corwin Press, Inc.

For information:

Corwin Press, Inc.
A Sage Publications Company
2455 Teller Road
Thousand Oaks, California 91320
E-mail: order@corwinpress.com

Sage Publications Ltd.
6 Bonhill Street
London EC2A 4PU
United Kingdom

Sage Publications India Pvt. Ltd.
M-32 Market
Greater Kailash I
New Delhi 110 048 India

Printed in the United States of America

Library of Congress Cataloging-in-Publication Data

Irby, Beverly J.
    The career advancement portfolio / by Beverly J. Irby,
Genevieve Brown.
        p.   cm.
    ISBN 0-7619-7541-1 (cloth: alk. paper)
    ISBN 0-7619-7542-X (pbk.: alk. Paper)
    1. Education—Vocational guidance—United States.
2. Employment portfolios—United States.   I. Brown, Genevieve.
II. Title.
    LB1775.2.172   2000
    370'.23'73—dc21   008084

This book is printed on acid-free paper.

00 01 02 03 04 05 10 9 8 7 6 5 4 3 2 1

Corwin Editorial Assistant: Kylee Liegl
Production Editor: Denise Santoyo
Editorial Assistant: Nevair Kabakian
Typesetter/Designer: Janelle LeMaster
Cover Designer: Oscar Desierto

Contents

Preface

Frequently, people who want to advance in their careers or change careers need assistance. As recognized authorities in career advancement strategies for leaders and in the development of administrator portfolios, we have mentored many job seekers in the development and use of a powerful career advancement tool: the career advancement portfolio.

The career advancement portfolio is powerful in two ways. First, the portfolio development process alters the way in which applicants view themselves, allowing them to recognize and capitalize on their strengths and minimize their weaknesses. Second, the portfolio changes the way employers determine the best applicant, as it provides critical information regarding the applicant's potential and fit for the position.

If you are about to begin a job search process, perhaps you are not looking forward to developing a portfolio. Perhaps it appears to be an overwhelming task, and if you are not certain of just how to go about it, trying to create a portfolio can be a frustrating and intimidating experience. The career advancement portfolio is designed to make developing your portfolio manageable and rewarding. The step-by-step process outlined in this book will enable you to create, in a sequential and stress-free manner, a career advancement portfolio that highlights your abilities and accomplishments and enhances your professional image.

Chapter 1 describes the career advancement portfolio and explains why job applicants have found it so helpful in marketing themselves. Chapter 2 provides step-by-step directions on how to begin portfolio development. In Chapter 3, you will learn how to articulate your beliefs and career goals and how to graphically demonstrate your unique experiences and skills. Chapter 4 offers specific suggestions for creating electronic career advancement portfolios. The directions and examples in Chapter 5 will enable you to create an attention-getting application portfolio, whereas Chapter 6 shares tips on using the portfolio to enhance your interview. In Chapter 7, you will find answers to five questions frequently asked about career advancement portfolios.

This book can support you in furthering your career goals, regardless of whether you:

- Are seeking your first leadership position
- Hope to move up the administrative ladder in your current school district
- Want to make a lateral move to gain varied experience in a related leadership area (e.g., if you are a grant director seeking to become a principal)
- Desire to change school districts but remain in the same type of position
- Wish to use your leadership experience in education in another field (e.g., if you are a technology coordinator planning to work for a computer company).

Begin by adopting the philosophy of career advancement portfolio proponents. Believe that as a result of analyzing your potential, clarifying your professional goals, and organizing documentation of your accomplishments in a logical and professional manner, you will become more confident and masterful in your job search and will be able to convince potential employers that you are the right person for the position.

Although time constraints do not permit us to povide readers individual assistance with career advancement portfolios, we would enjoy hearing about your experiences using career advancement portfolios. Please e-mail us at edu_bid@shsu.edu or edu_gxb@shsu.edu, or write to us at Box 2119, Sam Houston State University, Huntsville, TX 77431.

Publisher's Note: You may want to buy the companion book, *The Principal Portfolio*, published by Corwin Press, to acquaint yourself with other types and uses of portfolios.

Authors' Note: We are grateful to the many educators with whom we have worked on portfolio development and who have provided feedback and examples throughout the years. Special appreciation is due Sylvia Barnett, Carol Brown, Heath Burns, Jennifer Marcoux, Charlie Michel, Jodie Rhodes, Linda Rodriguez, and Angie Stallings.

About the Authors

Beverly J. Irby is Professor and Director of the Center for Research and Doctoral Studies in the Department of Educational Leadership and Counseling at Sam Houston State University. She also serves as a Title VII director for the Doctoral Bilingual Fellowship in Educational Leadership. At Sam Houston State University, she has served as director of field experiences, supervisor of mentor services, liaison for the urban profession development site, and as Title VII grant coordinator on an urban elementary school campus. She has also served as an elementary school principal, assistant superintendent, interim superintendent, school psychologist, educational diagnostician, and special education director. Her research, writing, and presentations have explored the principalship, administrative portfolio development, electronic portfolio development, general and women's leadership issues, personnel and program evaluation, program development in bilingual education, parent involvement, gifted education, science education, and adolescent pregnancy and parenting programs. She is the author or coauthor of numerous grants totaling more than $5 million and often serves as a consultant to school districts. She is a member of the International Who's Who of Women and has received the Texas Council of Women School Educators' Outstanding Educator Award and the Renaissance Group Research Fellow Award. The coauthor of *The Principal Portfolio* and *The Administrator Appraisal System*, she is cofounder and coeditor of *Advancing Women in Leadership Journal*, the first international, on-line refereed journal for professional women. She is also a coeditor or coauthor of six books on women's issues, including *Women in Leadership: Structuring Success, Women as School Executives: A Powerful Paradigm, Women as School Executives: Voices and Visions, The Teen Pregnancy and Parenting Handbook,* and *The Discussion Guide: The Teen Pregnancy and Parenting Handbook.*

Genevieve Brown is Professor and Chair of the Department of Educational Leadership and Counseling at Sam Houston State University, Huntsville, Texas. She has extensive experience as an administrator in public schools, including 10 years as assistant superintendent. Her research and writing, focused on administrative portfolio development, administrator career development, administrator evaluation, leadership theory, organizational structures, staff development, and equity issues, have been published in numerous books and journals. She is coauthor of *The Principal Portfolio* and *The Administrator Appraisal System*. She is coeditor of numerous books on leadership, including *Women in Leadership: Structuring Success, Women as School Executives: A Powerful Paradigm, Women as School Executives: Voices and Visions,* and *Supervision and Site-Based Decision-Making: Roles, Relationships, Responsibilities, and Realities.* She is also a coprincipal investigator of several grants and has served on numerous state and national organizations' executive boards. A frequent presenter at state and national meetings and consultant to school districts and universities, she is listed in the *International Who's Who*. She was recognized in Texas as Outstanding Instructional Leader and Outstanding Woman Educator and has received the Renaissance Group Research Fellow Award.

1

The Career Advancement Portfolio

Career advancement portfolios are being recognized as a necessity in the application and interview process by educators successful in advancing in their careers. These educators have discovered that the career advancement portfolio offers them a competitive edge as they seek leadership positions among a field of many qualified applicants.

Furthermore, employers support the use of portfolios in the educational leadership job search process. They report that portfolios yield valuable, in-depth information about applicants and that the person who presents a career advancement portfolio communicates a more professional image.

Developed with the ultimate goal of marketing oneself, the career advancement portfolio is a collection of concrete work examples (artifacts) and accompanying reflections that highlight leadership strengths and accomplishments.

The career advancement portfolio process enables applicants to:

1. Self-assess, determine strengths, and plan for growth
2. Showcase strengths in leadership related to the position
3. Learn more about the particular position, the school, and the district
4. Clarify their own values and beliefs and compare them with those of the organization

> *I will no longer interview an applicant without his or her career advancement portfolio because the portfolio gives me much more in-depth information about the individual. The information gained through the career advancement portfolio allows me to make better decisions in the hiring of new administrators.*
>
> —Principal C.

1

In the process of self-assessing and doing their homework about the position and the district, applicants learn more about themselves and determine their match with the position and the district and/or campus. Applicants state that they feel better prepared for the interview and more confident, and they attribute this preparedness and confidence to the process of portfolio development.

From carefully selected artifacts and thoughtfully written reflections and other items in the portfolio, interviewers gain important information regarding the applicant's philosophy, potential, experiences, skills, and strengths that might not otherwise be evident in the typical résumé, application form, or interview.

What is a Career Advancement Portfolio?

The career advancement portfolio is a collection of thoughtfully selected artifacts and reflections indicative of an individual's experiences and ability to lead related to an established set of leadership criteria or job-related functions. The career advancement portfolio is sometimes referred to as a professional or presentation portfolio. Much more than just a scrapbook or work examples, the career advancement portfolio differs from many job search portfolios in that it contains not only artifacts but also reflections.

Components of the Career Advancement Portfolio

The following are important components of the career advancement portfolio:

1. Table of Contents
2. Introduction
3. Résumé
4. Leadership framework
5. Professional goals
6. Leadership domains (includes artifacts and reflections)
7. Accolades

The sample table of contents in Figure 1.1 provides an overview of what is usually included in the career advancement portfolio. Chapters 2 and 3 describe each of these components in detail and provide examples and guidelines related to each.

Variations of the Career Advancement Portfolio

Successful applicants, we have discovered, not only tailor their portfolios to the particular job they are seeking but they also adapt the career advancement portfolio to various situations. We have assisted many candidates with developing what we call the *application portfolio*, which is a brief and concise introductory portfolio submitted with the application letter. Furthermore, we have encouraged applicants to go beyond the traditional paper portfolio to create and present electronic portfolios. Details regarding these variations of the career advancement portfolio are found in Chapters 4 and 5.

Why Develop a Career Advancement Portfolio?

Figure 1.1. Career Advancement Portfolio: Sample Table of Contents

Table of Contents

*Each domain includes artifacts and reflections

In the career development seminars that we have conducted, we find that individuals in a field of many qualified applicants are looking for a competitive edge, and the career advancement portfolio offers just that. Proven to be an effective tool for advancement within the district or for seeking positions outside the district, the career advancement portfolio (a) improves marketability; (b) demonstrates credibility; (c) demonstrates an understanding of the job; (d) assists with determining the "fit," and (e) provides employers a closer look at the applicant.

Improves Marketability

Our research with hundreds of developers of career advancement portfolios indicates there are many advantages. Perhaps the greatest career advantage is that it helps applicants in marketing themselves by highlighting strengths and accomplishments.

The career advancement portfolio offered me a way to organize my artifacts and think about or reflect on why those had been important in my development as a leader. I think this process really helped me to know myself better and to be better prepared for my interview. This is a great marketing tool!

—Assistant Principal R.

I was able to show how I had led the teachers in my district in curriculum revision in the content reading areas, and how this made a difference in the improvement of reading test scores. Because I had done this work in curriculum, it was easier for me to establish credibility in the area of curriculum development. Because I included this experience in my portfolio, I was able to obtain a district-level curriculum coordinator position.

—Principal J.

In the competitive field of school leadership, it is essential that administrators know how to market themselves. In the first place, job searches have become more complicated. For example, in many districts common practice is no longer just a single person interviewing; rather, it is a group of individuals, including parents, community members, teachers, other administrators, and the superintendent. (The interview team is often dependent on the position sought.) Because of this new structure in interviewing, it is incumbent on the administrator candidate to sell himself or herself to each individual. A career advancement portfolio greatly assists the candidate in this task. Through the development of the portfolio, the candidate has addressed a variety of leadership skills, making it easier to portray the comprehensiveness of his or her abilities and experiences and to convince the interview team of strengths.

Demonstrates Credibility

Another advantage of a career advancement portfolio is that it demonstrates one's credibility. It is difficult to successfully communicate the professional credibility necessary to secure the desired position simply through the application or interview process. The portfolio showcases leadership ability, professional reputation, and school and community involvement, thereby allowing the candidate to actually reconstruct the evidence of his or her track record in leadership.

Demonstrates Understanding of the Job

A key to obtaining a job is to be familiar not only with the district or campus but also with the specific job requirements. Tying the portfolio to the position being sought makes it much easier for the candidate to express his or her understanding of the expectations of the job and how his or her experiences relate to those expectations.

Assists With Determining the "Fit"

Related to the notion of understanding the expectations of the job, is finding the right fit. Because the applicant has developed his or her portfolio to align with the expectations of the job, he or she has become very familiar with the campus and/or district. In addition, the applicant has written his or her leadership philosophy through the leadership framework. These ac-

Figure 1.2. Advantages of the Career Advancement Portfolio for Applicants and Interviewers

Applicant	*Interviewer*
1. Captures visible evidences of leadership experiences and skills	1. Affords the interviewer real-world evidence of leadership and skills of the applicant
2. Enhances professional image	2. Offers a positive image of the applicant to the interviewer
3. Increases awareness of personal strengths and growth areas	3. Provides the interviewer concrete evidence of strengths and future plans
4. Enhances self-confidence of the applicant by better preparing him or her for the interview	4. Allows the interviewer to ask specific questions related to professional experiences
5. Assists the applicant in goal setting by allowing him or her to see where weaknesses exist and where growth is needed	5. Provides the interviewer with a glimpse of what the applicant views as important professionally through his or her goals
6. Clarifies values and beliefs related to learning and leadership	6. Gives valuable insights into leadership and educational philosophy
7. Provides opportunities to take control of the direction of the interview	7. Gives the interviewer additional information for further discussion in the interview

tivities are advantageous for the candidate in that he or she is able to determine the match between his or her experiences and philosophy and the district's and campus's job requirements and philosophy.

Provides Employers a Closer Look at the Applicant

Employers repeatedly report that they hired the person who presented a career advancement portfolio, or they indicate that that person made a great impression using the portfolio. A thoughtful, well-organized career advancement portfolio offers potential employers concrete representations of the applicant's qualifications and gives interviewers important information related to strengths, professional values and ethics, and problem-solving ability, providing prospective employers an accurate assessment of the applicant's credentials, accomplishments, and potential. Figure 1.2 lists advantages of the career advancement portfolio for both applicants and interviewers.

The benefits of the career advancement portfolio are numerous—not only to applicants but also to potential employers. Educators are discovering that the career advancement portfolio is an innovative and viable tool for pursuing initial leadership positions, seeking promotions, and assessing applicants.

2

Initiating Your Career Advancement Portfolio

Developing a career advancement portfolio that portrays you as the person most qualified for the position and that encourages utmost consideration by the reviewer involves the eight steps listed in Figure 2.1. This chapter discusses the first three steps.

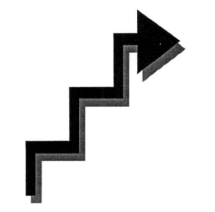

Figure 2.1. Steps to Portfolio Development

1. Determine the physical, organizational, and conceptual structure of the portfolio
2. Develop an introduction
3. Create or update your résumé
4. Develop your leadership framework
5. Articulate your professional goals
6. Select artifacts that illustrate your leadership capabilities
7. Write reflections to accompany the artifacts
8. Select artifacts for the accolades section

Appearance, Organization, and Structure

The portfolio should invite immediate review, be well organized, be professional and attractive, and should facilitate quick and easy location of each item. Arranging the portfolio in a zippered three-ring binder adds to the attractiveness and professional appearance of the portfolio and makes it easier for both the reviewer and the applicant to handle. The table of contents should list each section with page numbers. Sections in the portfolio, as indicated in Figure 2.2, should be clearly indicated by tabbed pages or color-coded divider pages. When typing the portfolio entries or section page dividers, give attention to the font size and style. Select an easy-to-read, professional font and do not change it unless the altered form is used for emphasis or adds to the attractiveness of the portfolio. Be sure that the divider page tabs lie outside the pages included in the portfolio. This facilitates easy identification of and access to each section.

I had developed a portfolio to use as I looked for a teaching position. I really fixed it up cute with clip art of children and little books—things like that. Now after I have finished a course on the development and use of the career advancement portfolio, I find that I must not make my portfolio for an administrative position "cutesy." I will make this one more professional, since I will be seeking an assistant principal position.

—Teacher M.

As you consider the conceptual structure of your career advancement portfolio, keep uppermost in your mind that the purpose of your document is to convince the reader or the interviewer(s) that you are the very best applicant for the job. You will need to determine in the early stages whether you will structure the artifacts and reflections section of your portfolio around general leadership domains (Figure 1.1 in Chapter 1 offers an example of this structure) or around the functions or duties listed in the job description of the particular position you are seeking.

Most administrative jobs, such as an assistant principal, principal, coordinator of curriculum, assistant superintendent of instruction, and so forth,

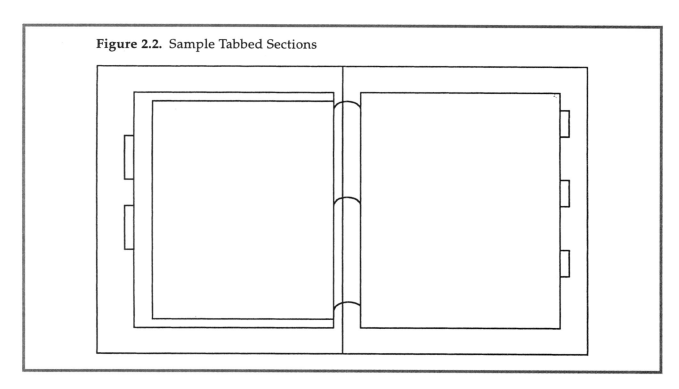

Figure 2.2. Sample Tabbed Sections

My first career advancement portfolio was sectioned into the state job proficiencies for administrators. My section pages and my divider tabs were hidden between pages in my portfolio. I noticed the reviewer had a hard time finding my various sections because of the hidden divider tabs. I corrected that before my next interview, and the review went much smoother.

—Assistant Math Coordinator F.

will have common general requirements such as competency in instructional management, fiscal management, or school and community relations. These commonalities will appear from district to district, and even from state to state. Several state and national organizations, such as the National Association of Secondary School Principals, the National Association of Elementary School Principals, and the American Association of School Administrators, provide general leadership expectations for leaders. In addition, most states have developed such criteria. Also, individual research results have yielded characteristics of successful leaders. Our own study involving more than 100 practicing administrators detected 25 administrative characteristics that employers look for in candidates. These characteristics are depicted in the rating scale shown in Figure 2.3. The items on this scale or similar leadership scales or criteria lists will be helpful in organizing your portfolio. Furthermore, rating yourself on this particular scale will assist you in identifying your leadership strengths and areas for growth. Once a portfolio has been developed based on commonly held leadership expectations, making minor modifications to fit a specific position is fairly simple.

Applicants with whom we have worked have indicated that they have had the best success with portfolios that are tailored to the specific job they are seeking. They have obtained the job description in advance and have either initiated their portfolio based on the qualifications of the job or have adapted a portfolio organized around generic leadership skills. Figure 2.4 is an example of an administrative job description and Figure 2.5 provides a sample portfolio structured around that particular position.

Components of the Career Advancement Portfolio

Each of the following six components outlined in Figure 2.5 is discussed in this chapter and in Chapter 3:

- Introduction
- Résumé
- Leadership framework
- Professional goals
- Job functions and responsibilities
- Accolades

Figure 2.3. Desirable Administrative Characteristics

Desirable Administrative Characteristics Rating Scale

Rate yourself on a 1 to 5 scale on the 25 characteristics listed below.

1 = excellent
2 = above average
3 = average
4 = below average
5 = needs improvement

Characteristics		Performance Rating				
Instructional						
1	Knowledge of teaching strategies	1	2	3	4	5
2	Knowledge of effective discipline techniques	1	2	3	4	5
3	Knowledge of and sensitivity to diverse populations	1	2	3	4	5
4	Knowledge of current trends	1	2	3	4	5
5	Commitment to student learning	1	2	3	4	5
6	Technology skills	1	2	3	4	5
7	Learning as a priority	1	2	3	4	5
Personal						
8	Integrity, loyalty, and honesty	1	2	3	4	5
9	Strong independent skills	1	2	3	4	5
10	Enthusiasm and energy	1	2	3	4	5
11	Professional appearance	1	2	3	4	5
12	Good judgment	1	2	3	4	5
13	Cooperative and positive	1	2	3	4	5
14	Openness to change	1	2	3	4	5
15	Sense of humor	1	2	3	4	5
16	Flexibility	1	2	3	4	5
Managerial						
17	Team player	1	2	3	4	5
18	Organized	1	2	3	4	5
19	Vision	1	2	3	4	5
20	Initiative	1	2	3	4	5
21	Strong communication skills	1	2	3	4	5
22	Creative problem solver	1	2	3	4	5
23	Positive public relations	1	2	3	4	5
24	Professional development	1	2	3	4	5
25	Leadership and success in current position	1	2	3	4	5

Figure 2.4. Sample Administrative Job Description With Broad Job Performance Areas

Executive Director of Curriculum and Instruction

Qualifications:
The executive director of curriculum and instruction shall: (a) have the qualifications of a teacher as prescribed by the State Department of Education, (b) hold at least a master's degree from an accredited college or university and a valid administrator's certificate, and (c) have had at least 5 years of successful teaching, administrative, and/or supervisory experience.

Job performance statements:
1. Instructional management
2. School climate
3. School improvement
4. Personnel management
5. Administration and fiscal/facilities management
6. Student management
7. School and community relations
8. Professional growth and development
9. Other

Figure 2.5. Sample Portfolio Outline

*Each job function/responsibiltiy includes artifacts and reflections

Introduction

The introduction will explain the purpose and organization of your portfolio, provide a brief overview of the contents, and function as an advanced organizer. It will also offer an opportunity to briefly introduce yourself as a viable candidate to the reviewer. The example in Figure 2.6 is tailored to a specific position and includes brief reflections and additional information.

Résumé

Résumés introduce you to the potential employer and are critical tools for marketing yourself. This initial paperwork makes a first and lasting impression and is essential to your securing an interview.

The interviewers with whom we have worked say that they consider the following when selecting applicants from résumés:

- Appropriate certification or licensure
- Experiences related to expectations of the position
- Experiences related to desirable administrative characteristics

Figure 2.6. Sample Introduction for the Position of Director of Curriculum Development

This portfolio offers me an opportunity to share with others my leadership accomplishments and experiences. A review of the table of contents will indicate that the artifacts and accompanying reflections are related to the job description of director of curriculum development and to the seven administrator standards set forth by the state. Although I have had many valuable experiences and have gained much knowledge in all areas of leadership, I believe my greatest expertise is in working with teachers to improve instruction.

My leadership framework demonstrates my strong commitment to fostering growth in teachers and students, and my professional goals include areas in which I plan to obtain additional knowledge, skills, or experiences during the next 5 years.

In summary, I believe that I have the skills and disposition to be a successful director of curriculum development in the Springdale School District, and I appreciate the opportunity to offer concrete representations of my experiences through this portfolio.

- Evidence of current training or workshops
- Experience, expertise, and training in key campus or district programs
- Professional, well-organized, easy-to-read format
- References

Prior to preparing the résumé, you will want to review the five steps in Figure 2.7.

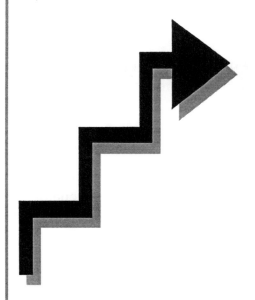

Figure 2.7. Five Steps in Preparing the Résumé

1. Reread the job description or the leadership criteria
2. Write down the most important duties, functions, and areas of concentration
3. List skills or special training necessary to perform the duties
4. State your own achievements or experiences in each leadership domain or function
5. List leadership expectations from Figure 2.3, or key personal traits important to the position, such as the following:
   - Child-centered
   - Follows procedures
   - Problem solver
   - Team player
   - Creative
   - Lifelong learner
   - Interpersonal skills

Figure 2.8. Worksheet for Résumé Development

Domain 1: Leadership and Campus Culture
- Chair of campus improvement team
- Training workshop in group processes

Domain 2: Human Resources Leadership and Management
- Chair of principal selection team
- Member of campus staff development committee

Domain 3: Communication and Community Relations
- Editor of campus newsletter

Domain 4: Curriculum Planning and Development
- Member of district curriculum committee
- Chair of campus curriculum alignment committee

Domain 5: Instructional Leadership and Management
- Fifth-grade team leader
- Mentor for four new teachers
- Peer coach

As you begin to develop your résumé, create an outline by listing actual on-the-job experiences that demonstrate your competence or knowledge in each area of the job description or in each leadership domain. Many people report that this helps them recall experiences significant in their leadership development that they perhaps had forgotten or had not realized were important. Figure 2.8 illustrates this process.

If there is a domain in which you do not have relevant accomplishments, you may have identified a gap in your experience. This is helpful in goal setting and in deciding what experiences you need to "get under your belt" for career advancement.

Listing your specific experience for the résumé will be helpful later as you assemble your portfolio. Refer to this worksheet as you consider artifacts to include.

Basic Rules of Résumé Writing

Length. We are frequently asked, "How long should my résumé be?" Although in the business world the recommendation is usually one or two pages, we have found that it is acceptable in the educational arena to have a longer résumé—four to five pages, including references.

Readability. You will need to generate your résumé on the computer, keeping it easy to read and understandable. Although you want your résumé to include words and phrases representative of expectations of the position such as those in the scale found in Figure 2.3, be careful to avoid overuse of jargon or buzz words.

Paper and font. Do not use flashy paper. You will want to use conservative colors of paper, usually white, gray, or ecru, and always use black ink. Choose a font that is easy to read and be consistent in your use of bolding or italicizing.

Language, grammar, and format. Be consistent with your language, punctuation, and format. For example, if you spell out months (September, 1999) or use numbers (9/99), be consistent. Be sure to proofread your résumé; it is also a good idea to have others proofread it. Errors on your résumé will immediately place you at risk of not making the applicant pool.

Accomplishments and experiences. Tailor the résumé to the position sought or structure the résumé around general leadership criteria or skills, emphasizing your achievements and experiences in areas critical to the position. In addition, be sure to include awards and honors, recent relevant training, and professional organizations of which you are a member.

References. The last page of your résumé will list your references. Be sure to select references who are totally supportive of your career and who are knowledgeable about your accomplishments, skills, and career potential. Ask permission to use their names and keep your references informed about your job search so they can provide reliable and accurate information about you. Include full names, titles, addresses, phone numbers, and e-mail addresses of the 3 to 10 references listed. We advocate arranging this important information into what we refer to as a *reference register*. The reference register lists names and addresses of individuals who can verify the specific examples of skills and experiences that you will be stressing in your portfolio. You will want to list the job functions or leadership areas once again and place the individual reference names under each function or area to which the individual can attest. Figure 2.9 displays a sample reference register.

The abbreviated résumé in Figure 2.10 includes a career objective and areas of concentration and strength clearly related to the objective. The objective personalizes the résumé to the specific job for which the applicant is applying. Although including a career objective on your résumé is not required, we have found that applicants and interviewers encourage it.

Another way that you might consider developing your résumé is to list your experience and responsibility by jobs you have had in the past. If you do this, be sure you list accomplishments that demonstrate qualifications related to the position for which you are applying. An example of how you might list this on your résumé is provided in Figure 2.11.

We often get another question, "Should we include a photo?" We respond, "It's best to leave it off." Photos can keep you from getting into the applicant pool. If you are already in the applicant pool and the résumé is part of the portfolio at that point, it is fine to include your photo.

Figure 2.9. Sample Reference Register

Instructional management
Ms. Jo Smith, Principal
Allen Elementary
203 Reed Road
Houston, Texas 77777
713-777-7777, e-mail:jsmith@txnet.edu.state

School climate
Mr. Tom Gee, Teacher, Chair of Campus Improvement Team
Rains Intermediate
345 Jones Road
Katy, Texas 88888
713-888-8888, e-mail: tgee@txnet.edu.state

Personnel management
Dr. M. Golding, Superintendent
Dancing Creek School District
4567 West Road
Tomball, Texas 99999
713-444-4444, e-mail: mgold@txnet.edu.state

School and community relations
Mr. H.T. Nelson, Manager of Happyland Foods
7890 Wirtson Road
Houston, Texas 88999
713-000-0000, e-mail: htnelson@happyland.com

Fiscal management
Dr. Franklin Dodd, Assistant Superintendent for Finance
Dancing Creek School District
4567 West Road
Tomball, Texas 99999
713-333-3333, e-mail: fdodd@txnet.edu.state

Figure 2.10. Sample Abbreviated Résumé

Louise Grantham
232 Gravel Hill Road
Houston, Texas 75555
713-555-5555

Career objective: To serve Black Hawk Public Schools by responsibly facilitating growth of professional staff as the director of staff development

Professional Qualifications, Education, and Additional Training

M.Ed.	University of Mississippi, University, MS, 1990
B.S.	Delta State University, Cleveland, MS, 1972

Certifications: Elementary Education, Special Education, Principalship

July 1995	Portfolio Development, Texas A&M University-Commerce, Commerce, TX
July 1994	Change Facilitation, SEDL, Austin, TX
June 1993	The Seven Habits of Highly Effective People, Covey Facilitator Training, Provo, UT
June 1989	Grant Workshop, Texas Women's University, Denton, TX

Chronological Employment History

August 1991 to Present	Principal, Williams Elementary, Katy Public Schools, Katy, TX
August 1988 to August 1991	Assistant Principal, Grenada Public Schools, Grenada, MS
August 1984 to August 1988	Team Leader, Special Education, Horn Lake Public Schools, Horn Lake, MS
August 1974 to August 1984	Supervisor, Sulpher Springs Public Schools, Sulpher Springs, TX
August 1972 to August 1974	Teacher, Louisville Public Schools, Louisville, TX

Areas of Expertise

- **Instructional management**
  - Supervised 100 language arts program teachers in a 7,000-member school district
  - Administered all special education curriculum programs in a 25,000-member school district, including 2500 students, 150 teachers, and 50 paraprofessionals
  - Led in the alignment of the curriculum as assistant principal at Tie Elementary School; resulted in increased test scores of 15% over a 2-year period

- **School improvement**
  - Organized the Campus Improvement Team to align goals, mission, curriculum, and parent and community involvement when principal; led to state recognition of the school 3 years in a row

(continued)

Figure 2.10. Continued

- **Personnel management**
  — Altered staffing patterns on the current campus to include music for all grade levels; upon retirement of one physical education aide and one office aide, I used this money and negotiated with the adjacent intermediate campus principal to split the cost of a music teacher who could provide services for all students at least once a week on both campuses
  — Reduced special education staff by 10% through ongoing staff development programs on least restrictive environment and regular classroom interventions over a 3-year period

- **Fiscal management**
  — Recognized by the Board of Trustees as the campus that allocated most funds to instruction; all funding goals or requests were directly tied to instruction as recommended by the Fiscal Management Committee under the supervision of the Campus Improvement Team
  — Garnered more than $2,000,000 in grant funds over a 10-year period to assist with professional development of teachers and to secure additional materials for classroom instruction

Professional Organizations

Texas Association of Supervision and Curriculum Development; Chair of Membership Committee, Texas Elementary Principals and Supervisors Association

Strengths

Team builder, student-centered, bilingual in English and Spanish, program evaluation, change facilitation, grant writing and acquisition (funded grants total > $2,000,000)

Figure 2.11. Example of How to List Previous Jobs With Responsibilities

The side heading on the résumé would be as follows:

Experience and Responsibilities

Good Day School District
Assistant Principal—Middle School   1992 to Present

- Assisted principal with personnel and staffing, including reviewing portfolios and interviewing candidates
- Developed growth plans with teachers for professional development
- Planned with teachers for instructional improvement
- Coordinated textbook inventory
- Administered discipline appropriately and equitably
- Served as administrative representative on ARD and 504 committees
- Implemented with campus team the District Strategic Plan and Campus Improvement Plan
- Introduced and implemented Peer Mediation Program
- Conducted teacher evaluations
- Developed master schedule and coordinated student scheduling
- Assisted principal with developing and monitoring campus budget

3

Completing Your Career Advancement Portfolio

You now should have your portfolio well underway. You have determined how it will be organized, written the introduction, and developed your résumé. This chapter will take you through the final five steps for completing your career advancement portfolio as outlined in Chapter 2: developing your leadership framework, articulating your professional goals, selecting artifacts that illustrate your leadership capabilities, writing reflections to accompany the artifacts, and selecting artifacts for the accolades section of your portfolio.

Leadership Framework

The leadership framework is a comprehensive analysis of primary beliefs and attitudes regarding students, teachers, schools, learning, and leadership. A personal leadership framework helps in clarifying *who* we are as leaders not only to ourselves but also to potential employers. All of our actions are predicated on our beliefs and values; therefore, it is important to know ourselves well and to express our beliefs clearly in writing. The leadership framework provides the first step toward better understanding ourselves as leaders, as it compels us to reflect on our philosophy of leadership, learning, and teaching. This self-analysis offers opportunities for personal and professional growth and prepares us to share our belief system with others.

A thoughtful, sincere, and well-written leadership framework affords portfolio reviewers important insights into the applicant. School leaders report that when they ask interviewees questions related to their philosophy or when they review written philosophical statements, they are looking for the potential employee's beliefs regarding issues vital to educational success, awareness of current leadership trends and issues, commitment to instructional improvement, concern for children and society in general, and for the applicant's "fit" with the campus or district belief system and mission.

Structured specifically to address these expectations, the leadership framework is more comprehensive than a general philosophy of education. The seven components of the leadership framework[1] and an explanation of each follow:

1. *Philosophy of Education:* This component provides insights into basic beliefs about the purposes of education and the importance of schools to society, forming the foundation not only for the leader's practice but also for subsequent components of the framework.

2. *Philosophy of Leadership:* What the leader believes about effective leadership and its impact is stated here. Questions such as "What constitutes effective, purposeful leadership?" and "How is effective, purposeful leadership sustained?" are addressed.

3. *Vision for Learners:* An in-depth analysis of what the leader believes about how children or adolescents learn and about his or her role in promoting learning is essential to the development of this component.

4. *Vision for Teachers:* Here the leader examines and shares his or her views on teachers; that is, what it means to be a teacher, what a teacher's role is in lives of children in the classroom and within the campus community, and how teachers should relate to students and others.

5. *Vision for the Organization:* A discussion of the leader's vision for the organization is important because this provides an image of what the leader thinks the district or campus should be or could be. Within this component, the leader should comment on the following:

    Climate

    Community

    Collaboration

    Communication

6. *Vision for Professional Growth:* This section details how the leader feels about the impact of professional growth on student achievement and effective schools. Here, the leader discusses his or her views on the significance of professional development for himself or herself and for the faculty as well as how professional growth needs will be determined and addressed.

7. *Method of Vision Attainment:* Without a strategy for obtaining the vision, visions are merely cryptic illusions. In discussing how he or she will move the organization toward the vision, the leader will need to address the following:

> Decision making
>
> Encouragement, initiation, and facilitation of change
>
> Support during change

To begin your leadership framework, jot down under each of the seven components thoughts that first come to mind. If you have written a general philosophy of education, reviewing it now might be helpful. After you have outlined some ideas, go back to each component and set aside some soul-searching time. It is important that your framework represents what you truly believe and how you will operate.

Remember that you want your leadership framework to be clear and free of excessive jargon and "high flown" or abstract terms, but at the same time you want your words and thoughts to express your attitudes related to significant issues in leadership and education. As you begin to elaborate and refine initial ideas, keep the language straightforward, but be sure that it reflects your beliefs about and your awareness of current leadership issues, challenges, and expectations.

Although the leadership framework should be comprehensive, it should not be lengthy. One or two brief paragraphs for each component is sufficient. Figures 3.1 and 3.2 offer examples of leadership frameworks.

Your leadership framework will also be helpful in writing reflections. In fact, it is actually the first written reflection in the portfolio development process. As you write reflections related to artifacts representing leadership accomplishments, you will want to make sure that your reflections are congruent with your framework.

An additional benefit of the leadership framework is that it encourages self-analysis and reflection critical to growth. This will be discussed later in this chapter.

> *I believe the panel really read my leadership framework. One member commented that they were glad I had so clearly articulated my vision of equity and excellence, and another said that he was impressed that I had talked about moral leadership.*
>
> —Assistant Superintendent W.

Figure 3.1. Example of Leadership Framework

Leadership Framework
Rosalinda Lara
Science Department Chair
Wells Middle School

Philosophy of Education

There are two major functions of education. The first function is to provide students with basic tools to be productive in society. Therefore, schools should provide students with the education they need to become self-sufficient and an employee or employer in the future, rather than a burden to society. The second function is to motivate students to be the best that they can be and hire a staff who is there for the student and who believes "the child comes first."

Philosophy of Leadership

As a future assistant principal, I feel the Human Resource Model is most effective. It is important to provide teachers with the tools needed to have an effective classroom. I also believe in instilling a safe, positive, and comfortable environment so that for students and teachers alike, "school is a place you love to come to and regret to leave." However, as an administrator, I must ensure that teachers are effective in the classroom.

Vision for Learners

Every child deserves a well-rounded education. This encompasses not only an education in the classroom but also extracurricular activities, teamwork, the development of personalities, and the social aspect that a school can provide.

Vision for Teachers

Teachers are motivators, facilitators, and a vast source of knowledge to their students. Teachers have a lasting effect on the life of a child, which is an awesome responsibility. Teachers should be positive and share the philosophy that the child comes first through relationship building. Teachers should have the time to plan and brainstorm to address the different learning styles and needs of students and be the most effective they can be.

Vision for the Organization

My vision for the school as an organization revolves around the four "Cs": climate, community, collaboration, and communication. The climate of the school should be a safe and positive environment, a place you love to come to and regret to leave. The community should be directly involved in the school through parent organizations so they feel a sense of ownership and pride. There should be constant collaboration between students, parents, teachers, and administrators. Communication is the key to any successful organization, and as an effective assistant principal, it is important to uphold the open-door policy.

Vision for Professional Growth

For myself, I believe professional growth is an ongoing process that is developed every day. Relationship building is part of this growth. It is important to build relationships between students and teachers. This opens the lines of communication. As an evaluator of teachers, I would like them to feel free to focus on one aspect a year in an area in which they feel they need growth. It is then important to shift to the role of facilitator in helping teachers reach their goals that help them achieve that growth.

Method of Vision Attainment

My vision is making school "a place you love to come to and regret to leave." It is important to find teachers who buy into this vision, and then to empower them to attain the vision. It is essential for the school to have the dedication and confidence of the neighborhood communities as well as the local business community. Only when I have the full and total cooperation of all participants in the school community can the vision be attained.

Figure 3.2. Example of Leadership Framework

Leadership Framework
Carol Greenberg

Philosophy of Education

I believe that a good education is imperative for the well-being of our young people. It is important that they learn how to use their own abilities, problem solve, work with others, and serve as responsible citizens of a democracy. These are skills and attitudes that we as educators must help instill in them in order for students to live productive, satisfied lives.

Philosophy of Leadership

The principal sets the tone for the entire building, and I always try to lead by example with a positive attitude of encouragement. Just as I want teachers to afford students an environment in which to grow steadily and safely, I want teachers to feel free to try new things and feel safe in communicating openly with me. We are a team working together for the betterment of our precious students.

Vision for Learners

Students come to us with a great diversity of prior knowledge, learning styles, economic stability, and parental support. We must create a learning situation that takes into account all these differences. Lessons must be relevant to the students, and students must feel safe to try new things. Emphasis needs to be on critical thinking, an essential lifelong skill.

Vision for Teachers

I have great admiration and respect for teachers. They have a difficult, yet tremendously rewarding, job. They are definitely the key to successful learning for students. A teacher's positive relationship with the students cannot be overemphasized. That, coupled with an enthusiastic, well-prepared lesson unfolding in the safe classroom makes a tremendous impact on students.

Vision for the Organization

The school should be a place where staff and students are actively engaged in the process of learning. Everyone should be focused on the goal of helping students become lifelong learners. Parents and community members are an invaluable asset in this teamwork that is needed to help make every child successful. Open communication is vital to this exciting endeavor.

Vision for Professional Growth

Just as it is definitely essential for the principal to continue to grow professionally, it is also essential that he or she helps teachers grow professionally. Relevant staff development that is planned and presented by building teachers can be a very effective learning tool. So, too, can opportunities for teachers to observe each other teaching. Furthermore, it is important for building representatives to attend workshops and then share new techniques and strategies with staff. Administrators and teachers should be models of lifelong learners for students.

Method of Vision Attainment

A clear mission and teamwork are vital to the success of all of our students. Only through open communication and a leader with a positive, encouraging attitude can this occur. Building relationships will be the cornerstone in dealing with students, staff, parents, and community members. This should never be used as a substitute for academic excellence, but rather as a bridge that helps one attain the goal of excellence in learning. Most people thrive in a supportive environment where there are high expectations, and the principal, as a positive role model for excellence in education, can guide the school to tremendous success.

Professional Goals

The inclusion of professional goals in the portfolio conveys to prospective employers that you know where you need to go and that you have a plan for getting there. The importance of creating a written plan cannot be overemphasized; when goals are written, there is a tendency to accomplish them. As you begin to develop your goals, look back at the job description and your résumé. Helpful questions include the following:

- What are my personal administrative plans for the next 5 years?
- Where do I see myself in the future?
- Where do I see my organization in the future?
- What contributions do I see myself making?
- What is important to me in my profession, and how can I accomplish this through a 5-year plan?
- In what areas would I like to expand my expertise or pursue further training?

I've always had goals and a plan in my head, but it wasn't until I got really specific and put on paper how I would accomplish my goals that I was able to see my growth.

—Secondary Principal R.

Goals of a school principal might include those outlined in Figure 3.3, and another example of professional goals can be found in Figure 3.4.

Figure 3.3. Example of Professional Goals

Within the next 5 years, I plan to accomplish several goals related to the principalship:

1. Access funding for additional technology and technology training for campus teachers and myself

2. Provide conversational Spanish classes to my teachers, and take Spanish immersion classes in Mexico during the summer. Close to this goal is to provide cultural sensitivity training for the teachers and myself as well

3. Form study teams on my campus for investigating a systems-thinking approach to curriculum development

4. Obtain experience as a principal at the middle school and high school levels

Figure 3.4. Example of Professional Goals

- Ensure a positive school climate where teachers, students, parents, and the community are valued
- Increase academic performance in order to become an exemplary campus
- Facilitate and support the continued implementation of the St. Johns Intermediate School campus plan
- Facilitate and support the continued implementation of the Grandville District Strategic Plan
- Design and implement a successful alternative to social promotion for fifth- and sixth-grade students
- Support the continued implementation of the electronic curriculum that is aligned vertically and horizontally to maximize student success
- Obtain a principal position
- Continue my professional growth as a lifelong learner

Artifacts

Artifacts and reflections are the heart of the career advancement portfolio. It is in this section that you will provide concrete examples of the leadership accomplishments or experiences that qualify you for the position and will, through reflections on those accomplishments, demonstrate your expertise and ability to analyze the impact of your actions and determine necessary next steps in your growth as a leader.

If you are not in the habit of keeping samples or concrete evidence of your work experiences, you will need to begin to do so immediately. Certificates, agendas of meetings, brochures, or newspaper articles you have written are all potential artifacts. As you begin your artifacts collection, set up file folders for each domain, function, or criteria of leadership or for each of the specified duties of the particular position you plan to pursue. You might want to look back at Figure 1.1 in Chapter 1 or Figure 2.3 in Chapter 2 for listings of leadership domains or areas that would be relevant to most administrative positions. These will make good headings for your file folders if you are not yet ready to create folders related to a particular position. If you have already determined the position you will pursue and have obtained a copy of the job description, file folder labels should reflect each of the job's expectations. Figure 3.5 illustrates several file folder titles related to the director of elementary curriculum position with sample artifacts.

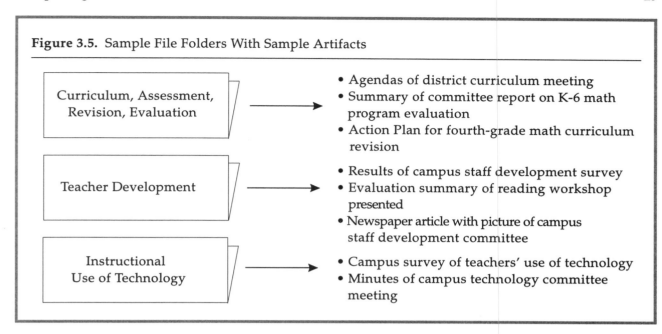

Figure 3.5. Sample File Folders With Sample Artifacts

Curriculum, Assessment, Revision, Evaluation →
- Agendas of district curriculum meeting
- Summary of committee report on K-6 math program evaluation
- Action Plan for fourth-grade math curriculum revision

Teacher Development →
- Results of campus staff development survey
- Evaluation summary of reading workshop presented
- Newspaper article with picture of campus staff development committee

Instructional Use of Technology →
- Campus survey of teachers' use of technology
- Minutes of campus technology committee meeting

Look through your existing files, notebooks, and so forth and drop in the appropriate file any specific item or relevant notes. Keep your folders in view and close at hand so you will be reminded to document your experiences and so you can easily make additions.

You may find it helpful to look back at your calendar entries to recall past activities that might be significant. Checking with others who participated in those activities to see if they have copies of particular items that might be appropriate could also be beneficial. Be sure to file any items that you have developed or participated in that might be useable. It is not yet time to discriminate; you are trying to build a collection from which you can later select the very best representations.

Once you have a sufficient collection, you will begin the all-important selection process. Because of time constraints of reviewers, it is essential to limit the number of artifacts that you include in your career advancement portfolio. This is definitely a situation in which less is more; remember, you are aiming for quality, not quantity.

You will select only one or two artifacts for each leadership criteria or job function, and it is critical that you select those items that best demonstrate your leadership competence, showcase your accomplishments, and attract the attention of potential employers. The reflection cycle, to be discussed later, offers helpful prompts for artifact selection.

> *I developed an academic portfolio during my principal certification program. I immediately began a career advancement portfolio even though I wasn't ready to apply for an assistant principalship. I rearranged my sections based on the job description, and I was able to use some of those artifacts as well as my leadership framework. I also set up a file folder for each job function and began collecting artifacts. It was much easier than starting from scratch.*
>
> —Assistant Principal P.

Figure 3.6. Leadership Criteria and Complementary Artifacts

Leadership Criteria	Artifacts
1. Instructional management	Copy of report related to the performance of a group of students including an analysis and interpretation of data
2. School climate	Collaboratively developed plan for enhancing the professional growth and socialization of beginning teachers and mentors
3. School improvement	Campus improvement goals, revision, and evidence of accomplishment
4. Personnel management	New staffing patterns based on input from all faculty members after study groups analyzed systematically the curriculum, instruction, and budget
5. Administration and fiscal/ facilities management	Facilities study conducted by consultant with input from faculty and staff members

Sample leadership criteria and a complementary artifact for each criterion are listed in Figure 3.6.

Reflections

Reflections, for the purpose of the career advancement portfolio, are written accounts of the engagement in thoughtful and careful analysis of past practices and experiences with the transformation of the analysis into a future action or goal. Our research has indicated the need for a structure for writing reflections about artifacts. The reflection cycle (see Figure 3.7) provides such a structure and offers critical prompts.[2]

The reflection cycle offers a structure and allows for individuality while ensuring that critical aspects are addressed. The steps are intended to serve as a general outline, and the suggested questions serve as prompts to assist in the actual writing of the reflections that will accompany the artifacts in the portfolio. As you move through the stages of reflection, you may not necessarily answer every question.

Step 1: Select. As explained previously, you must first select the artifacts most representative of the leadership proficiencies that you are attempting to demonstrate. In this step you will ask the following:

What documents or artifacts most graphically represent my involvement or activities in this particular job function?

Figure 3.7. The Reflection Cycle

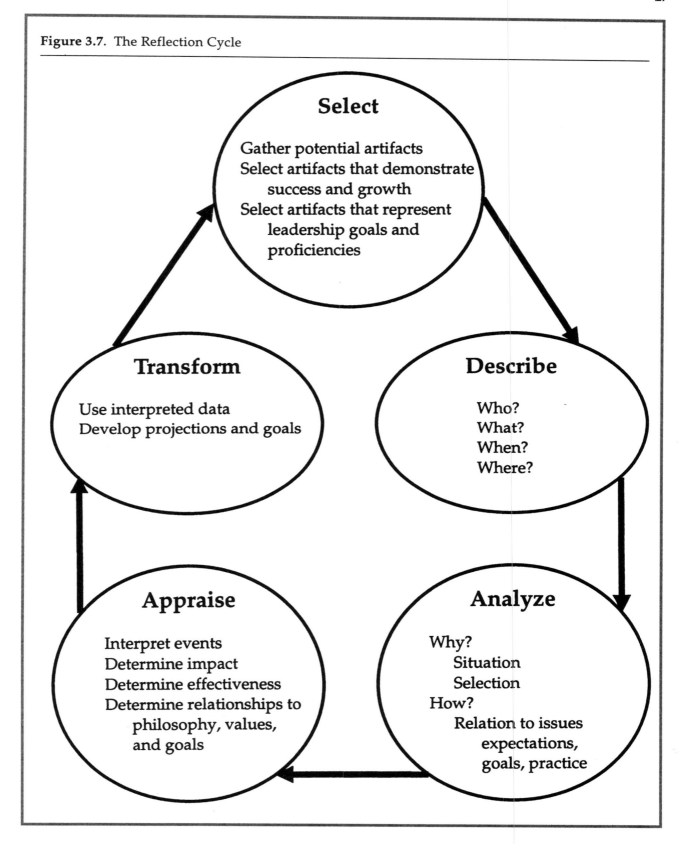

Select

Gather potential artifacts
Select artifacts that demonstrate
    success and growth
Select artifacts that represent
    leadership goals and
    proficiencies

Transform

Use interpreted data
Develop projections and goals

Describe

Who?
What?
When?
Where?

Appraise

Interpret events
Determine impact
Determine effectiveness
Determine relationships to
    philosophy, values,
    and goals

Analyze

Why?
    Situation
    Selection
How?
    Relation to issues
        expectations,
        goals, practice

> Which artifacts relate directly to the goal or proficiency and demonstrate success and/or growth?
>
> Which artifacts best showcase my capabilities or skills in this area?

Step 2: Describe. A description of the circumstances, situation, or events related to the experience is included in this step. The following four *W* questions are usually addressed:

> *Who* was involved?
>
> *What* were the circumstances, concerns, or issues?
>
> *When* did the event or series of events occur?
>
> *Where* did this take place?

Step 3: Analyze. This step involves "digging deeper." The *why* of the selection of the artifact and the *how* of its relationship to the events, leadership skills, issues or beliefs, circumstances, and/or decisions occur. Appropriate questions include the following:

> *Why* is this artifact representative of the specific job function?
>
> *Why* is the situation represented in this artifact significant in demonstrating competency in this area of responsibility?
>
> *How* does this artifact relate to:
>   —personal, district, or campus goals?
>   —leadership expectations, skills, or beliefs?
>
> *How* is the vision developed and shared?
>
> *How* is collaboration facilitated?
>
> *How* is feedback provided and received?
>
> *How* are resources managed and organized?
>
> *How* are plans developed and implemented?
>
> *How* are decisions made and acted on?

Step 4: Appraise. In the previous three steps, you have described and analyzed the experience. The actual self-assessment occurs in Step 4 as you interpret the events, evaluate the impact and appropriateness of your action(s), and relate them to your values and beliefs. Suggested guiding questions are the following:

Did the action(s) taken result in the intended outcomes?

Were the actions effective and appropriate in the situation?

Were the actions consistent with my leadership framework?

What impact did decisions or actions have on students, teachers, and/or the community?

Is this leadership behavior representative of district expectations?

Were options derived from multiple perspectives considered?

Were a variety of alternatives considered?

Was the very best course of action taken?

How might this situation have been approached in a different manner? What types of results might be expected?

What action(s) might have resulted in a more positive impact?

How does this experience promote growth?

Step 5: Transform. This step holds the greatest opportunity for demonstrating your vision and your leadership potential at the next career level. Ask yourself the following questions:

> How can I demonstrate that my actions and decisions could move the organization beyond standard expectations related to the job function?
>
> What future activities could I engage in that would enhance my leadership skills and practice?
>
> How could my experiences help to improve practice (my own and teacher's)?
>
> What plan for improvement of student learning can be developed from the interpreted experiences?
>
> Has reflection resulted in a need to alter my leadership framework?

My experiences related to fiscal management assisted me in securing the director of financial operations position. I wrote my reflection on the computerized process I developed for requisitions and budget monitoring on my campus. I also was allowed to pilot this on three other campuses. In the appraise section of the reflection I reported the results of the study I did on the efficacy of the system. In the transform section I explained how I would move this to the district level by training staff systemwide.

—Principal G.

The reflections in Figures 3.8 and 3.9 illustrate the use of the five steps in the reflection cycle.

Reflection necessitates engagement in thoughtful and careful analysis and reporting of past practices, events, experiences, and future considerations. Reflection will assist you in moving from a basic level of acceptance of the way things are in the process of schooling to a level of critical examination and self-assessment. New visions of yourself also result from reflection. In the transform step of the reflections you will communicate to potential employers your ability to transfer leadership experiences you have had in one position to the position you are seeking.

Accolades

An accolade is any artifact that denotes an accomplishment. Your goal in this section is to provide to the reviewer evidence of your credibility with colleagues, supervisors, students, parents, and the community. You will want to include certificates or newspaper articles related to honors or awards or recognitions you have received; letters or notes of commendation, gratitude, and support; and/or evaluations of outstanding performance.

Figure 3.8. Reflection for Learner-Centered Climate

The artifacts that I selected to demonstrate my accomplishments in this proficiency are as follows:

1. New teacher inservice agenda   (SELECT)
2. Substitute teacher inservice agenda
3. Bilingual/ESL Parent Program certificate

1. New Teacher Inservice Agenda August 9, 2000	2. Substitute Teacher Inservice Agenda August 10, 2000	3. Lideres del Futuro! This is to certify that
A. Welcome Principal J. B. Review of campus plan	A. Welcome B. Lesson plans C. Discipline referrals	_____ has successfully completed the program.

The first artifact is important because it indicates my understanding and belief   (DESCRIBE)
in communication, motivation, and team building. New teachers to the profession need to be
socialized into the profession and need to be mentored. This is our first step in the process. I
schedule the mentors and mentees and pair the two for the campus. This is critical to the continued positive climate of the school and the well-being of the teaching profession.

The second artifact represents my commitment to the positive climate on the campus and district. The substitute teachers are critical extensions in the teachers' absences; therefore, I believe that the inservice for them is important to make sure they have been acclimated to the district and campus life.

The third artifact represents my commitment to the parents of our students. This is one program among many that we provide. I developed the concept of the ESL parent   (ANALYZE)
training programs 5 years ago while at Sammons through the grant I wrote, Queremos Triunfar.
The current program has been extended to a new grant, Lideres del Futuro. The provision of
the Saturday classes to assist parents in developing their English skills, computer skills, and
parenting skills has been successful in projecting a positive climate in the community. Teachers
are involved in this project and help to develop the curriculum and instruction for the parents.
I arranged the day care for the students.   (APPRAISE)
Many accolades were given to the Caroll faculty and staff during the final ceremony represented by this artifact. Parents indicated that through this program they were able to better
themselves and ultimately their children.

In opening a new school, developing a positive climate in the community and   (TRANSFORM)
on the campus as a total team involvement is extremely critical. All the diverse cultures must
be taken into account as the school mission is implemented. I understand culture and climate
and the dynamics of change; I will continue to take these into account as we provide a safe, secure, and nonthreatening environment for the young learners on the campus.

Note: The example artifacts are not placed the way we would recommend they be placed in a portfolio. Artifacts
should be on separate pages across from or following the reflection. These were designed to save space in this
text.

Figure 3.9. Reflection for Learner-Centered Communication

The three artifacts I selected for this proficiency reflect my commitment to communicate effectively, openly, and honestly. They are:

1. Carroll Academy Handbook

Carroll
Academy
Handbook

2000-2001

2. Parent Training Brochure

3. Newspaper article

The first artifact represents my ability to communicate in writing effectively and my ability to use technology in my written communications. I revised the Carroll Faculty Handbook and shared the policies with the teachers.

The second artifact reflects both written and oral communication to parents. I initiated this program in which parents were trained to assist children with their reading. This program empowered parents to communicate with their children through reading and speaking.

The third artifact reflects my commitment to successfully promote public relations through the Bilingual Homecoming program. The purpose was to make the parents and students feel welcome back to their neighborhood school for bilingual education. Prior to this, students had been bused to other sites. Parents of 87% of the students attended the Homecoming. Evaluations indicated that they felt welcome and that they would be comfortable participating in similar meetings. This program represents my ability to plan and conduct effective meetings, problem solve, facilitate a team for a common cause, and develop positive public relations. I plan to develop other such programs in the future, and I will sponsor a similar program for the grand opening of the Early Childhood Center.

Note: The example artifacts are not placed the way we would recommend they be placed in a portfolio. Artifacts should be on separate pages across from or following the reflection. These were designed to save space in this text.

Figure 3.10. Examples of the Types of Accolades to Include in the Career Advancement Portfolio

---

- Certificate of Appreciation for Service on the State Task Force for Secondary Science
- Area newspaper article reporting receipt of grant for teacher staff development in teaching higher-order thinking skills
- Letter of congratulations from the superintendent for being named area Principal of the Year
- Letter of support from the language arts teachers at Spring Woods Middle School for facilitating curriculum revision efforts
- Letter of commendation from the president of the local Rotary Club for the outstanding presentation of the middle school technology program

---

It is not necessary to write reflections to accompany the artifacts included in the accolades section, and, once again, remember to limit the number you include. Keep the time and interest of the reviewer in mind and include only those few examples (five to eight) that document your skills and abilities as perceived by others, demonstrate that you are well thought of by those with whom you work, and if possible, which relate to the position you are seeking. Figure 3.10 lists the contents of the accolades section of a person applying for the position of director of elementary curriculum.

Additional Thoughts on Portfolio Development

You will want to ask yourself the following questions as you finalize your career advancement portfolio:

- Will my portfolio stand out in a crowd?[3]
- Does the length of my portfolio invite review by busy school administrators, teachers, or parents?
- Does my portfolio clearly reveal my philosophy of leadership?
- Do my portfolio contents relay to the reviewer my philosophy about teaching, learning, and/or schools?
- Is my vision for students and staff evident?
- Does my portfolio provide the reviewer with evidence as to how I manage and organize resources, time, and people?
- Have I presented myself as a person of integrity and credibility?
- Have I overlooked any opportunity to demonstrate competence through my portfolio?
- Does my portfolio show that my qualifications are a match for the position I am seeking?
- Does my portfolio represent my best effort in written communication (grammar, style, spelling, etc.)?

Once you have determined the answers to these questions and made modifications as necessary, you will want to have colleagues, supervisors, and/or professors analyze your portfolio with these questions in mind. Developing a simple checklist from these questions for use in the analysis is helpful.

Remember that portfolio development requires commitment. As the examples provided indicate, it takes time, energy, and thought to develop or update your résumé, leadership framework, and goals; select the appropriate artifacts that will demonstrate your competency to the reviewer; and reflect and write those reflections so that the reviewer gets a clear picture of your professionalism and your potential for the position you are seeking. Successful candidates have informed us that the time, energy, and effort involved in the development of their career advancement portfolios clearly is worth it when they consider the benefits that they derive.

Notes

1. Taken from Brown, G., & Irby, B. J. (1997). *The Principal Portfolio.* Thousand Oaks, CA: Corwin.

2. Taken from Brown, G., & Irby, B. J. (1997). *The Principal Portfolio.* Thousand Oaks, CA: Corwin.

3. This does not mean that your portfolio needs to be cute; rather, to "stand out in the crowd" means that you have included in your portfolio items that truly showcase the strengths you bring to the position.

4

The Electronic Career Advancement Portfolio

Although hard-copy or paper portfolios continue to be the type most widely used for career advancement, more and more educators are discovering that electronic career advancement portfolios are a compelling means through which to display their unique skills and expertise to prospective employers. Information regarding the development of this electronic tool for marketing oneself can be a valuable addition to the repertoire of a technologically adept school leader.

The purpose of the electronic portfolio is the same as that of the traditional paper portfolio: to showcase your abilities and accomplishments as you apply for educational leadership positions.

Including all that a paper portfolio includes, the electronic portfolio offers the following special advantages not only to the candidate for the position but also to the prospective employer:

- Ease of use
- Efficient use of space and storage
- Ease in updating and replacing materials
- A multimedia format
- On-line accessibility

Furthermore, the electronic portfolio demonstrates to potential employers the technological expertise of the creator.

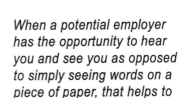

When a potential employer has the opportunity to hear you and see you as opposed to simply seeing words on a piece of paper, that helps to give an edge in the pursuit of that job.

—Assistant Principal B.

Electronic career advancement portfolios may be produced in one of the following three formats: a Webfolio, a Hyperstudio® Folio, or a PowerPoint® Folio.

Webfolio

The electronic career advancement portfolio may be developed via a Web page on the World Wide Web. Incorporating technology into the career advancement portfolio to create a webfolio not only provides potential employers with easy and convenient access to the most recent information about you, but it also indicates to these professionals what you know and what you can do related to the electronic medium.

Although webfolios are not the current trend in the world of educational administration, we believe that they will gain in popularity as educators discover their benefits. Webfolios can:

1. Demonstrate currency in the use of technology
2. Allow for creativity in inclusion of images, sounds, video, and text
3. Easily adapt from traditional paper portfolios
4. Provide the potential for employers to respond directly to the applicant via e-mail that would be included in the webfolio
5. Allow for e-mailing of the portfolio to all interview team members without a lapse in time as is the case with regular post
6. Make a person "alive" and "real" to a prospective employer
7. Portray the candidate much more vividly than can the written text
8. Motivate adults to learn new computer skills or to work collaboratively to develop the new skills

Two sample career advancement webfolio front pages are found in Figures 4.1 and 4.2. Webfolios can be developed using a variety of Web page development software products and linked to a host site. Such software may

---

Tips for Making a Webfolio

1. Create your Webfolio with the potential employer in mind.
2. Make your Webfolio easy to use.
3. Use a type/font that is easy to read. Use three sizes of fonts: headlines, subheadlines, and body. Do not use all capital letters.
4. Pick colors and backgrounds that are easy to see. Limit the number of colors to four.
5. Use pictures, images, video clips, and sound to support your text. Remember, every picture you add will increase the time it takes to download the pages.
6. Include a mail-to (e-mail) link so reviewers can contact you easily.

Figure 4.1. Sample Webfolio Front Page

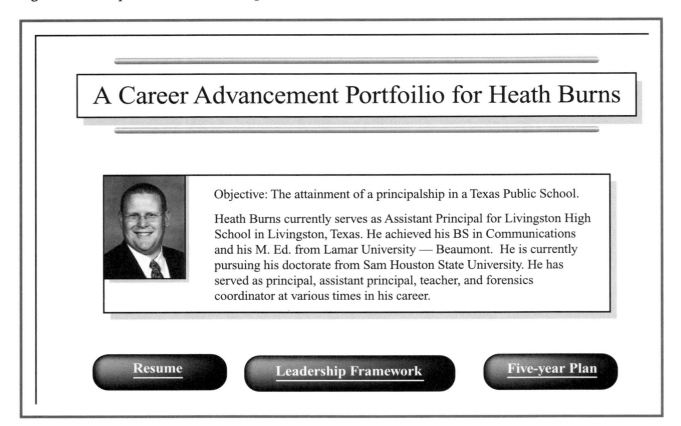

be purchased at office supply or computer software stores. Usually, a school district has a host server on which your webfolio can be housed; however, you may want to consider using another host if you are considering applying outside your current district. A note of caution: If you use video clips on webfolios, be reminded that they are slow to download (25K is the recommended size for ease of downloading).

Hyperstudio® and PowerPoint® Folios

Another medium or format in which an electronic career advancement portfolio can be developed is through authoring or presentation software such as Hyperstudio® or Microsoft PowerPoint®.

These electronic career advancement portfolios may be placed on a regular 3.5 inch disk, a zip disk, or a CD-ROM. An advantage of the use of the disk is that your career advancement portfolio may be duplicated and a disk left with each member of the interview team. Another advantage that we have found is that aspiring administrators have been able to use video

Figure 4.2. Sample Webfolio Front Page

Angela Stallings

Resume
Leadership Framework
Texas Administrator Proficiencies
Certifications
Miscellaneous

clips on CD-ROMs to demonstrate their skills. For example, one principal included brief clips of herself conducting a strategic planning meeting. A superintendent applicant had a clip of himself conducting a community information meeting on a bond issue. Applicants have also used the video clip as a way of introducing themselves and their portfolio or to share a part of their leadership framework or their goals. This makes the applicant "come alive" or may remind the prospective employer of something the candidate said during the actual interview as the portfolio is reviewed in virtual reality.

Suggestions for the
Development of Electronic Portfolios

Most applicants have developed a paper portfolio first and have then converted it to an electronic portfolio. However, if you are beginning with an electronic portfolio, the following specific suggestions will be helpful:

1. When beginning your electronic portfolio, develop working folders just as you would if you were creating a paper portfolio. The folders will hold artifacts and reflections related to job-specific functions or leadership proficiencies. Artifacts in the folders will include scanned documents such as newspaper clippings, letters, front pages of curriculum documents, agendas, and video clips. For the webfolio, these documents would be loaded into a web folder in the final development phase so links could be established.

2. Keep the electronic portfolio simple and easy to use; use the same icons and try to use those that appear professional. The reviewer should not have to try to figure out the software or where you have placed items on your page. Just as you have an introduction in the hard copy of the career advancement portfolio, you will also have one in the beginning of your electronic portfolio. You may include a table of contents, but hotlinks or buttons on your electronic portfolio may serve like a table of contents, guiding the reviewer. Examples of links that you may develop are Résumé, Leadership Framework, Professional Goals, and Leadership Proficiencies Including Artifacts and Reflections. These named links are simple and understandable.

3. The portfolio should be developed in a common platform. Of course, the webfolios would basically operate in any platform; however, if you are developing another type of electronic portfolio, the platform would be of concern.

4. Software version issues can be overcome by using runtime modules. Save the presentation in a presentation-only format, which creates a runtime module that a person can run on his or her computer without the actual software or concern about software versions.

5. The electronic portfolio should be easy to maintain with minimal upkeep time (approximately twice the time it takes to update your résumé).

6. The electronic portfolio should be user friendly.

7. Portfolios should include multiple forms of electronic multimedia such as static text, graphic displays, links if it is web-based, audio, photos, animation, recordings, and/or video clips. On the webfolio, be sure to limit these graphics, as large "Kb" graphics take time to download.

8. Graphics should be saved in "gif," "tiff," or "jpg" format, not in "bmp." Bit mapped (bmp) files are very large in size. Graphics saved as "bmp" cannot be displayed from web pages. A downside to "jpg," "gif," or "tiff" is that you will lose some crispness of the graphic.

9. Just as in the case of the hard copy version, the electronic career advancement portfolio should be kept at a length that would invite review.

Legal Issues Related to the Webfolio

The law does not prohibit employers from defining qualifications necessary for the position, but it does require that certain standards or qualifications for hiring be applied alike to all persons regardless of race, color, religion, sex, national origin, handicap, age, or ancestry. Because of these hiring standards, you may want to use caution in providing your webfolio URL address to potential employers, particularly if you have included a photo or video clips on your site. Providing visuals prior to your invitation for the interview may eliminate you from consideration; the potential employer may consider you not old enough, too old, or not the right sex or ethnicity for the position.

Security Issues Related to the Webfolio

If you are concerned with security issues, you may need to consider not using a webfolio. Individuals other than the potential employer may open your site. You may not want to put your physical address, addresses of references, and so forth on the site. It is possible, of course, to design your webfolio without personal contact information or information on your references. You might state that these could be provided upon request. The employer should be able to obtain this information from the application materials you submitted earlier.

Final Thoughts About the Electronic Career Advancement Portfolio

Electronic career advancement portfolios are beginning to emerge as a competitive and marketable format for presenting one's accomplishments. As our population becomes computer savvy and turns to technology to solve problems more frequently, it behooves applicants to, at the very least, view the electronic portfolio as a possible means for gaining that all-important competitive edge.

5

The Application Process

To present your portfolio, whether paper or electronic, you must "make the paper cut" and get an interview. Your letter of application is critical; it will likely determine whether you receive serious consideration as an applicant. You should develop a stand-out letter of application that garners attention and communicates your interest in and qualifications for the position.

The letters of application in Figures 5.1 and 5.2 will give you some ideas; however, remember that your letter should communicate your own personality, uniqueness, and abilities.

Many successful applicants have created an application portfolio to submit with their letter of application. The application portfolio is a much-scaled-down version of the career advancement portfolio. It is limited to no more than 12 pages and includes the following:

1. Letter of application
2. Table of contents
3. Résumé
4. Leadership framework
5. Position reflective brief

Basic Rules for Letters of Application

- Keep the letter to one page.
- Highlight experiences and accomplishments that relate to the position.
- Briefly state what you would bring to the position.
- Comment on your future plans and your leadership style or personal values or traits.

Figure 5.1. Sample Letter of Application

Gwendolyn Archer
Rt. 1, Box 425a
Richardson, Arkansas 22331

December 2, 1999

Dr. Johanna Sapphire
Superintendent
Richardson ISD
11143 Beltline
Richardson, Arkansas 22332

Dear Dr. Sapphire:

I am submitting this letter as my official letter of application for the position of principal at Richardson West High School. Although my résumé will provide you with a general outline of my educational and work experiences, problem-solving abilities, and some achievements, also please find listed experiences and skills that I believe are particularly suited for this position.

Applicable skills/experience/characteristics:

- Fifteen years in public education
- Nine years administrative and supervisory experience (campus)
- Appraised teachers at all levels
- Trained in the Effective Schools Research, supervised the Campus Improvement Planning process, supervised student teachers
- Demonstrated ability to motivate people to greater visions
- Developed and organized model staff development programs
- Directly responsible for federal budgets
- Presented at major conferences; developed exemplary programs recognized by the state department of education
- Secured and administered numerous topical grants
- Worked harmoniously with school communities, administrators, parents, students, and staff

In addition, I am able to be creative with moving matters along and providing the leadership necessary to ensure that quality programs are provided to our students. The services that we could provide to the students in the district are only limited by how far we dare to dream. All that we do in school should be for the betterment of the education of the children that we will ultimately serve.

My leadership style is the dynamic, assertive, shirt-sleeves type that exhibits a willingness to get the job done along with the ability to communicate, motivate, and inspire those around me to a team spirit. I am one who wants to learn, grow, and be successful, and I am not satisfied with "satisfactory."

I am enjoying my service at the school district and wish to further serve our students and school children in our area. Thank you for the time that you and the committee will be giving to my consideration for the position of principal. I look forward to hearing from you.

Sincerely,

Gwendolyn Archer

Figure 5.2. Sample Letter of Application

February 1, 2000

Dr. Jennifer Samuels
Superintendent
Happy Day ISD
Post Office Box 2453
Happy Day, Wyoming 77437

Dear Dr. Samuels:

I am very interested in the position of principal of Washington Middle School. After our telephone conversation, my mind started working immediately on possible ideas for discipline management plans and for developing positive parent involvement, and how this change should occur within the next several years, as change is a slow process. This is an exciting opportunity for me to work collaboratively on developing programs rather than working in a district where the programs have already been established.

The experience that I have had through serving on our Campus Advisory Committee and through sponsoring student council and Model United Nations has helped me establish strong working relationships with students, parents, and the community. I have also been very involved with technology. I have implemented technology into my daily lessons and have shared my techniques with others within my department and on my campus. I have also presented at the Region 6 Special Population Conference, and I have been asked to present to Idaho State University faculty for the Writing Across the Curriculum program using Hyperstudio as a writing tool. In addition, I have been asked by Holly Wells Schools to conduct a one-day staff development session about the integration of technology into the curriculum and how to use technology with writing.

The highlight of the past year was the receipt of a $5,000 grant for the Social Studies Department at Huntsville High School. We have used these funds for staff development and curriculum revision. I am including a portion of my portfolio on the disk enclosed, and I have also included a disk to use with Hyperstudio player. I plan to bring my portfolio to share with you and your team at the interview.

I have much to contribute to Happy Day ISD and consider this a wonderful growth opportunity. I am looking forward to meeting you and the interview team to discuss serving as Washington's next principal.

Sincerely,

Karen Lugo

Position Reflective Brief

Although artifacts and reflections are not included in the application portfolio, it does briefly describe, through the position reflective brief, accomplishments and future plans related to each function of the job description. The position reflective brief, arranged in three columns horizontally on the page, is a succinct version of your résumé, artifacts, and professional goals. The first column lists the duties specified in the position job description. In the second column, relevant experiences are aligned to each of the listed job duties. Reviewing your artifacts will give you ideas for this column. The third column denotes specific plans for professional development or actions to be taken related to the job duties. Your professional goals will be helpful here. Figure 5.3 contains four pages of a position reflective brief from an application portfolio.

Developing this brief offers another opportunity to assess your experiences against the expectations of the job and to determine your readiness and "fit" for the job. In the application process, you will have gathered information about the district or campus beyond just the job description. This information will assist you with comparing your brief and your leadership framework with district and campus philosophies, goals, expectations, and practices. Do you fit in this position, in this district, or on this campus? Does the district's philosophy match that which you have espoused? Other questions to consider in determining your fit are listed in Figure 5.4. Be sure to investigate any "red flags" and determine if you can live with them.

Your application portfolio should be in a thin black, dark blue, or brown portfolio binder that can be purchased at any office supply store. This type of plastic portfolio is not a ring binder; rather, it is very thin (1/4") and is made all in one piece. (Do not use a binder with brads or a spring clamp.) It has approximately six plastic sleeves inside. Put your printed pages in so that you are using the back and front of the sleeves. A maximum of 12 pages of print will be in the six plastic sleeves of your application portfolio. Insert blank pages in the front and back sleeves if you are short of pages of print. A sample of this type of application portfolio is shown in Figure 5.5.

> *There was a very large pool of applicants for the position. I got an interview. At the end of the interview, I was told by the Director of Personnel that my submitted materials [application portfolio] were very impressive.*
>
> —Assistant Principal M.

Figure 5.3. Sample Position Reflective Brief

Specific Duties (listed from job description of principal)	Evidence of Accomplishment (accomplishments are aligned with indicators from job description)	Future Plans (areas of growth or plans to improve are aligned to the indicators as applicable)
I. Instructional Management		
1. Cooperatively plans with Campus Advisory Team (CAT) and faculty members in the selection of materials, development of methodologies, and implementation of innovative teaching techniques, strategies, and staff development sessions	Served on CAT for 3 years at the elementary and secondary levels. Chaired student achievement Campus Improvement Planning (CIP) Committee (1994). Served as CIP facilitator (1993) and assisted with and/or coordinated writing and development of high school CIP (1996-98)	
2. Assists teachers in the daily operation of instruction	Teacher observations and periodic walk-through observations; beginning-of-year goal-setting conferences, midyear progress conferences, and end-of-year summative conferences	
3. Contributes to the implementation and continuous evaluation of the curricular/instructional program and personnel; recommends improvements in the purposes and design of the instructional programs related to the mission/goals of the school	Assisted in the development of the high school evaluation model to determine effectiveness of curriculum Conducted a statistical study of the effectiveness of an Algebra 1A/B block instructional program, and offered opportunities for faculty members, parents, and students to offer ideas, suggestions, comments, and criticisms through the use of annual surveys, grade-level assemblies, faculty meetings, and individual conferences	Workshop on Program Evaluation, 2000 Continue to disseminate and evaluate results of surveys (which will be modified to meet the needs of any school of which I become principal) Dissertation topic is "The Effects of Block Scheduling on Student Success"

II. School/Organization Climate

4. Has a clear sense of the school's mission and goals; initiates, interprets, and communicates supporting school programs and policies to promote a learner-centered environment	Through faculty meetings and carefully planned staff development sessions, the mission and vision were frequently revisited and program innovations and modifications were discussed to be certain our path was constant	In the school to which I am named principal, work with the faculty to keep the vision in the forefront (and adjust as necessary due to changing school needs) Maintain high visibility in the classroom
5. Facilitates and maintains an environment that is conducive to positive staff morale, collegiality, team building, and staff involvement in decision making directed toward improved student performance	Biweekly faculty meetings team building activities, and staff development	
6. Communicates effectively with students, staff, parents, and community	Weekly team leader meetings, biweekly faculty meetings, periodic faculty information updates, student assemblies, daily announcements, fall & spring Open House, parent orientation	Maintain availability for conferencing Get to know the new faculty and staff Continue community involvement; seek parent and teacher input into ways of increasing this involvement
7. Facilitates effective resolution of conflicts in a timely fashion	Daily contact with students, parents, and teachers who require assistance and guidance during conflicting situations	Enrollment in Conflict Resolution Strategies course during fall
8. Communicates and promotes high expectation levels for staff and student performance in an enabling, supportive way; provides recognition of excellence and achievement	School assemblies, straight-A student recognition, Student of the Month recognition, awards ceremony	Continue modeling positive attitude toward school and the teachers and students

Figure 5.3. Continued

Specific Duties	Evidence of Accomplishment	Future Plans
(listed from job description of principal)	(accomplishments are aligned with indicators from job description)	(areas of growth or plans to improve are aligned to the indicators as applicable)

III. School Organizational Improvement

9. Facilitates the building of a common vision for school improvement with the school community, goal setting, planning activities, and program implementation	Helped to develop and deliver staff development on campus goal setting Assisted in the development of and participated in a book review session on *Your Child's Growing Mind* by Jane Healy, Ph.D. (discussed issues from birth through adolescence)	Pursue additional innovative and effective staff development techniques through observation, workshops, and research. Work with the faculty to keep the vision in the forefront (and adjust as necessary due to changing school needs)
10. Identifies, analyzes, and applies research findings (e.g., effective school research correlates) to facilitate school improvement	Assisted in the development and implementation of "Spelling Counts" program, assisted in the implementation of study hall guidelines so all students would have the opportunity to receive time and assistance with their homework.	Provide direction through appropriate and effective staff development, monitoring, and assessment Continue to provide and receive ongoing feedback to and from individual teachers and departments
11. Develops (as necessary), maintains, and uses appropriate information systems and records necessary for attainment of campus performance objectives (Academic Excellence Indicators)	Developed and delivered most of the staff development (with the topics being chosen so that they were in line with district objectives and the high school CIP and vision)	
12. Evaluates and uses effective recommendations of the CAT with the sole purpose of improving the instructional program and/or staffing patterns	Used instructional technologists and instructional specialists to provide staff development to selected teachers depending on need (i.e., science/soc. student teachers received instruction on reading in the content areas and development of writing rubric)	Work with CAT team and faculty members to develop goals and objectives that promote student learning as well as the vision of the school

IV. Personnel Management

13. Interprets and communicates the school's mission, goals, and its supporting programs and policies

    Using teacher appraisal, assisted in the development and implementation of growth plans; provided documentation of improvement (growth) as well as that which was needed to support nonrenewal of contracts

    Receive training in the appraisal instrument used by my employing district so that I may more effectively provide feedback to all teachers in a manner commensurate with the district mission, vision, and procedures

14. Uses developmental supervision and appraisal instruments appropriately and ensures that evaluations clearly and accurately reflect staff performance

15. Confers with personnel regarding their professional growth and inservice training opportunities to develop and accomplish improvement goals

    Using same evaluation process, document exceptional performance by teachers who consistently go above and beyond in the areas of personal and professional growth as well as their overall teaching performance

16. Clearly defines expectations for staff performance regarding instructional strategies, classroom management, and communication with the public

17. Encourages personal and professional growth and leadership among the staff; recognizes exemplary performance

18. Is effective in interviewing, selecting, and orienting new staff; makes sound recommendations relative to personnel placement, transfer, retention, and dismissal

    Review personnel applications, select the best candidates, set up the interview as well as the interview committee, conduct the interview, and recommend the best applicants for employment

47

Figure 5.4. Questions to Consider When Determining Your Fit

Do the expectations of the position fit with your leadership framework, your experiences, and your expertise?

Do the priorities and culture of the campus and district fit with your leadership framework?

Does your leadership style complement the position?

Will you be able to work productively with the staff?

Can you grow professionally and personally in this position and in the district?

Can you make significant contributions toward the goals of the organization?

Figure 5.5. Sample Application Portfolio

Applicants who have mailed the application portfolio to prospective employers report that they were selected for an interview because of this document. Some successful applicants have taken several application portfolios to the interview and left them with the individuals on the interview team. Several candidates have suggested that they would place the application portfolio on a disk and mail it; we are currently gathering data from potential employers as to how well this method would be received.

According to applicants and employers, the application portfolio has the following advantages:

1. It communicates sincere interest in the job, as it reflects more time and effort than a simple application letter and résumé

2. It gives far more information about the applicant than just an application letter and résumé

3. It provides potential interviewers with possible questions

4. The inclusion of the leadership framework enables prospective employers to determine whether the applicant's philosophy complements that of the campus or district

5. It makes the paperwork of the applicant stand out in the pool

6. It demonstrates organization and creative ability

7. It demonstrates that the applicant has a thorough knowledge of the job and how his or her experiences correlate

8. It indicates that the applicant has thought about professional development and future plans

9. It enables the prospective employer to determine quickly whether the applicant's related experiences meet expectations

> *I got many job interviews because of my application portfolio. I am confident that I would not have even gotten my foot in the door in some of the districts if it had not been for this. I was able to select the best position for me because of the many interviews I got. In fact, every time I submitted it, I got an interview.*
>
> —Special Education Director

6

Maximizing the Interview Through the Career Advancement Portfolio

Much advice on interviewing is readily available in books and articles, and all share a major theme: Projecting a professional image is the key to a successful interview. Our research indicates that projecting confidence is also important. The career advancement portfolio has proven to be tremendously beneficial in helping candidates project confidence and professionalism during the interview.

Developing your career advancement portfolio greatly enhances your preparedness to answer questions confidently during the interview. For example, you will be well prepared to discuss your philosophy about education and leadership, a topic that typically comes up in an interview. Having developed your goals, you also will be prepared to answer another frequently asked question, "Where do you see yourself 5 years from now?" You will be able to directly refer to your résumé and artifacts in your portfolio as you are asked questions concerning your work experience and qualifications. Your poise and ready answers will communicate that all-important confidence and professionalism in interviews.

As you are developing your career advancement portfolio, you are reflecting on your experiences and finding evidences of your accomplishments in specific job-related areas. Candidates tell us again and

> By the time I had completed my portfolio and studied the information I had collected on the district, I was convinced I was perfect for the job. I shocked myself during the interview because I was able to answer all the questions so easily; I even added quite a bit about my related experiences. I'll always be convinced I got the job because I knew myself, the position, and the district so well, and I was able to articulate that.
>
> —Director of Human Resources

again that as they collect their artifacts and write their reflections, they are surprised at how much they have accomplished related to the expectations of the position. This certainly is a confidence booster.

The reflection process not only helps you to find your strengths, but also helps to determine your growth areas. Perhaps you realize that you have limited or no experiences in the area of fiscal management; obviously, that is a weakness for most leadership positions. Knowing this prior to going into the interview, you would be prepared to answer a question related to financial management, should it arise. In fact, we recommend that candidates prepare and practice ahead of time responses to questions that might come up related to anything that might appear to be a gap in experience or expertise. Furthermore, because you have found that finance is an area of need, you will have developed a professional development goal related to finance. Other goals would also be developed out of this process of reflection. Being able to articulate your goals during the interview portrays you as a professional and a continuous learner, whereas identifying your growth areas and clarifying how you will address them relieves interview anxiety and further enhances confidence. Several confidence boosters are listed in Figure 6.1.

Figure 6.1. How the Career Advancement Portfolio Boosts Confidence

1. Helps prepare you to answer questions confidently
2. Prepares you to discuss your philosophy with ease
3. Reveals your strengths and growth areas prior to the interview
4. Clarifies your professional development goals
5. Identifies specific expectations of the position and how your experiences and skills match up
6. Builds confidence through self-analysis and reflections on past experiences
7. Offers a prompt during the interview
8. Provides concrete examples for use during the interview
9. Helps you to determine and articulate your fit within the district or campus

---

Prior to the interview, you should have gathered vital information about the district and/or campus. Specifically, you will want to study the district's philosophy, mission, and goals. You will also need to analyze the campus and/or district improvement plan and district and campus ratings related to state or national testing. All of this information, plus your reflections related to the job expectations, helps you to determine your fit for the position prior to the interview, increases your confidence, and communicates professionalism.

Interview Questions and Responses

Research indicates that several topics reoccur during interviews for school leadership positions. The most frequent include the following:

1. Your preparation for the position
2. Your leadership style
3. The strengths and weaknesses you bring to the position
4. Your reasons for seeking the position
5. How you would implement change
6. Your philosophy regarding student discipline
7. Your vision for parental and community involvement
8. Your vision for teacher involvement, development, and motivation
9. Your expertise and experience in curriculum

You will be able to address any of these issues with confidence; everything you need is in your portfolio! Because you have reflected on and written about these topics as you have developed your portfolio, you will appear well prepared and professional as you respond.

Knowing you will be able to turn to the appropriate section of your portfolio as you discuss your answer also builds confidence. For example, Topics 2, 3, 6, 7, and 8 are addressed in your leadership framework. Topics 1 and 9 are included in your résumé. Your artifacts, reflections, and goals provide information for Topic 4 and enhance other topics as well.

Three of my principal friends volunteered to form a panel and conduct a mock interview with me. We even made a video tape of it. Although they asked some really tough questions, I felt I was more-or-less able to control the interview because there was always something in my portfolio I could refer to. Their feedback was very positive, and watching the tape enabled me to polish some things. When it came time for the real thing I felt totally ready and at ease. That practice paid off because I got the job!

—Assistant Principal C.

Prior to the interview you will want to practice talking about each of the items as you refer to your portfolio. We urge administrator applicants to compose or borrow interview questions and ask colleagues or supervisors to conduct a mock interview with them so they may become familiar with referring to their portfolio in their responses. All interviewees report that this greatly increases their confidence.

Most interviews also include some situational questions to ascertain how the applicant would solve problems or address issues. Although this is frightening to some because it is difficult to predict exactly what will be asked, these questions usually revolve around incidents dealing with discipline, angry parents, crises or safety issues, incompetent teachers, or increasing student achievement. Consider these as you are developing your portfolio. If you have experiences or training related to any of these issues, include those artifacts and write an accompanying reflection. Then prepare to refer to your portfolio as you answer. Because your answer to many of these situational-type questions will depend on your values, beliefs, and leadership style, you will also want to refer to your leadership framework.

Figure 6.2. Examples of Responses to Concluding Interview Questions

---

- Your newsletter states that all the principals in this district have participated in your Leadership Academy. As you will notice here in Section 3 of my portfolio, I am a certified 4-Mat trainer. Was this a part of the district leadership training?
- The reading scores on this campus indicate a dramatic rise. As assistant principal I had responsibilities for staff development for reading teachers. As you will note on page 11 of my portfolio, we implemented Success for All and had great results. To what do you attribute your increase in performance?
- As this artifact and reflection indicate, I chaired the 3-year curriculum alignment project on my campus. We found it to be a very rewarding and successful experience. Are the teachers on this campus currently involved in curriculum revision?
- Yes, I do have something I would like to share regarding my commitment to and my strategies for improving school climate. As you will see from Section 3, each spring we conduct an Organizational Health Survey on each campus and develop an action plan for the coming year. Both professional and paraprofessional staff are extremely pleased with what we have done to raise morale and create a sense of shared mission. I look forward to bringing this experience and expertise to Shady Grove.

Interviewers say that they always ask a concluding question such as, "Do you have any questions?" or "Do you have anything you would like to add?" Always respond, "Yes." This indicates that you have been listening and thinking and that you are prepared. Furthermore, this is another opportunity for you to sell yourself and offer concrete examples of your expertise by referring to your portfolio. We encourage candidates to use a three-step process in preparing for this part of the interview. First, review the job description along with information you have collected on the campus or district and make a list of questions that come to mind. Next, look through your portfolio and determine how you might relate each question back to your own experiences. Third, decide what you would like to add if given the opportunity. Write that down and find the appropriate section of the portfolio to which you will refer. Figure 6.2 offers suggestions.

Presenting the Portfolio

Administrators and prospective administrators have presented the portfolio in the interview process in a variety of ways. Following are several options for when and how to present the portfolio in the interview setting:

I submitted my portfolio in advance of the interview so that the interview team could have a more complete picture of my experiences and expertise prior to the interview. It really seemed that the panel members' questions were based on information in my portfolio. They were very impressed, and the superintendent said that it really allowed the interview team to begin to assess the match between my philosophy and skills and the school's expectations and needs.

—Coordinator J.

1. Submission in advance of the interview. Frequently, applicants have been requested to submit the portfolio in advance of the interview so that the interviewer or interview team may have a more complete picture of the applicant's experiences and expertise prior to the interview. Recall that some applicants submit an application portfolio with the application materials. Interviewers explain that reviewing the portfolio in advance assists in designing appropriate questions for individuals. In addition, this preview allows the interview team to begin to assess the match between the applicant's philosophy and skills and the school's expectations and needs. Of course, with the electronic portfolio, you can simply provide the URL web address or leave a disk or CD-ROM with the individual(s) with whom you are to interview. One administrator stated,

> I dropped my portfolio off the day before the interview took place. During the interview the panel members turned to different sections quickly and directly and asked me questions. They said they appreciated having time in advance to review it and to formulate questions ahead of time.

When I arrived for the interview and was introduced to the group, I noted that I had a portfolio with me that would provide them with a snapshot of my background and accomplishments. They requested that I pass the portfolio around during the interview, and questions were often asked based on the information presented in the portfolio. When the interview was complete, the chairperson asked if he could keep my portfolio for a few days so that he could thoroughly review its contents. Each person who interviewed me seemed impressed with the fact that I had a portfolio and with the contents.

—Principal G.

2. Informal review during the interview. Applicants have also made their portfolios available for review during the interview. Interview team members have requested that the portfolio be passed around during the interview so that interviewers might ask clarifying or probing questions related to portfolio contents.

3. Presentation during the interview. Some applicants report that they have made a brief, formal presentation of their portfolio's contents at the beginning of the interview as they introduced themselves to the team or individual interviewer. Several interviewers point out that one has to be cautious with this approach because of the time constraints in an interview setting. Although suggesting that on some occasions it may be possible to schedule in advance the time for a brief overview of the portfolio, interviewers stress that even this "scheduled portfolio time" would be limited to 6 to 10 minutes.

One administrator applicant related,

> When I walked in for the interview, I put the portfolio in the middle of the table and explained what it was and the different parts. I told the interview team (five people) that they should feel free to glance through it as I was speaking and that I would be referring to different artifacts and my leadership framework throughout the interview.
>
> When I was asked about my personal strengths, I referred them to my awards and honors section and briefly talked about recent professional development seminars and conferences I had attended. In answer to the question about why I was applying for the position, I referred them to my goals section and my plan for career advancement. I also worked in my artifacts as real-life examples for other questions.
>
> At the end of the interview, I asked them if they had any questions about anything they saw in the portfolio. They were all very complimentary of it.

> *I presented my portfolio as soon as I walked into the conference room. I said that I had it with me and would like to share it. I believe this is necessary because it can allow the questions to revolve around the portfolio.*
>
> *—Lead Teacher T.*

The scenario in Figure 6.3 shares how an applicant used both her paper and her electronic portfolio to her advantage during an interview.

Figure 6.3. Scenario: Sample Use of the Career Advancement Portfolio

I brought an actual hard copy of my portfolio and a disk containing my electronic portfolio to the interview. (I left the disk with the superintendent.) Of course, it was extremely important that I was thoroughly familiar with the categories and contents of my portfolio. I had been taught that if the portfolio were properly compiled, then the majority of the questions during the interview process could be answered using the portfolio.

Before the interview, I made sure that I had the equipment needed to present my electronic portfolio during the interview. At the beginning of the interview, I made the appropriate greetings and then asked the interviewer to insert the disk into his computer. He opened the file accordingly. Of course, I had a hard copy of the portfolio on the table in front of him positioned so that he could see it.

As a question was asked of me, I referred to a particularly related portfolio section and commented on it. For example, when the interviewer asked me about my educational philosophy, I referred to the leadership framework on my electronic portfolio and simultaneously disclosed it in the hard copy—all as I told the interviewer about my philosophy. At times the interviewer chose a button to click on the electronic portfolio and would ask me about this certain experience.

At the end of the interview, I thanked the interviewer and suggested that he keep my electronic portfolio for a day or two in order to answer any additional questions that he might have about my qualifications.

About 3 days later, I went back by the central office and picked up my portfolio. I got to see the interviewer again and thanked him one more time. The interviewer stated that he was impressed with my electronic portfolio and it really gave him greater insight into my abilities.

(I got the job!)

I was interviewed for an assistant principal's position by two of the administrators and the counselors at Ford Middle School. When I was asked a question regarding my strengths, I pointed out three of the artifacts in my portfolio. They then asked about my weaknesses. I really never had to answer that because I turned to my goals section and just explained what my goals were and how I planned to accomplish them.

—Supervisor P.

At the end of the interview of the panel members asked if there was anything I would like to add or ask. At that time, I walked the interviewers through my portfolio, highlighting sections that pertained to areas about which they questioned me. This kept the flow of the interview steady and allowed me to finish on a strong point.

—Assistant Principal B.

4. *Example during the interview.* Other applicants have used the portfolio during the interview but have not made a presentation nor passed the portfolio around. Keeping the portfolio themselves, they have pointed out particular examples or artifacts to enhance an answer to a specific question. For example, when one applicant was asked about her experience in planning, designing, and conducting staff development activities, she opened her portfolio to the staff development section that contained several staff development agendas as well as workshop participant evaluation summaries. Not only was she able to elaborate on the answer, but she was also able to discuss a specific workshop that she knew was needed on that particular campus, quickly and easily providing concrete examples of her success.

5. *Concluding the interview.* An applicant who used the portfolio at the end of the interview stated,

> Because the interview panel's format was very structured, I was unable to present my portfolio within the interview. I saved it until the end. This was a good way to leave a favorable impression with the interview team. Questions like, "What would you like to tell us about yourself?," "What do you consider to be your most rewarding accomplishment?," and "Is there anything you would like to ask us?" gave me the opportunity to point out particular portfolio items and to steer the interview towards the information I thought was most important for them to know in order to see me as a strong leader.

6. *Leave the portfolio with the interview team.* Some applicants report that they have briefly referred to their portfolio during the interview, but rather than presenting it or pointing out specific examples, they have simply left it for later review by the interviewer(s). This approach has also yielded positive results. Candidates state that picking up their portfolio later provided them an opportunity for a follow-up visit with the interviewer or the head of the interview team. All candidates report that the interviewer made positive comments or asked additional questions after having reviewed the portfolio.

A word of caution: It is important to be sensitive to the norms and expectations of the application process. You do not want to be perceived as being overbearing or intrusive in sharing your portfolio. District and campus procedures for interviews vary; ascertain guidelines in advance so that you will be able to gauge the appropriate time and method for sharing your portfolio.

Of the hundreds of applicants with whom we have worked, all have indicated positive results from developing and presenting their portfolios. They concur that it is a viable career advancement tool and they feel confident and prepared for the interview and for the position. More than 80% of the hundreds of interviewers we have consulted respond favorably to the use of the portfolio. They report that the career advancement portfolio is interviewer-friendly and that it greatly assists in selecting the top candidate from the pool. They also say that those who interview using a portfolio come across as better prepared a, onend more confident and professional.

7

The Career Advancement Portfolio

Questions and Answers

When should I begin my career advancement portfolio?

The answer is *now*! Perhaps you feel now is not the time to seek a new position. Although it may not be the best time to make a career move, it *is* the best time to begin your career advancement portfolio.

Many applicants who have been successful in obtaining the position they were seeking say that they started their portfolios well in advance of the job search process. Some were able to adapt their academic or course portfolios required in undergraduate or graduate course work. Others simply started from the beginning. They began by writing or revising their résumés, developing their leadership frameworks, and setting up a filing system for artifact collection. Beginning the portfolio before it is needed affords plenty of time for planning, collection, and reflection.

Is it possible to develop a portfolio that could be used for several different positions?

The career advancement portfolio, like the résumé, is a marketing tool. Just as you tailor your résumé to a particular position, you should do the same with the career advancement portfolio. Once you have created a well-thought-out and professional-looking career advancement portfolio for one position, it is not difficult to adapt it for another, as many educational leadership roles require the same general skills and knowledge areas.

Of course, your résumé would need to be modified for the particular position you are seeking, and some adaptations might need to be made to the portfolio's organizational structure. For example, if you have named the sections based on the specific duties of one position, you would need to revise your table of contents and divider pages to reflect the new position.

Many applicants report that they are usually able to use the same artifacts and simply revise the reflections to emphasize particular points. Adaptations may also need to be made to the goals and, perhaps, to the accolades section.

Is the development of a career advancement portfolio worth the time and effort required?

Successful applicants and their employers affirm the tremendous value of the career advancement portfolio in the job search. Benefits to both applicant and interviewer have been enumerated. Probably the greatest benefits reported are the self-awareness and the self-confidence that result from the process. Frequently, applicants remark that they felt so secure in the knowledge that they were qualified for the position and so well prepared for the interview that they were able to project far more confidence than they had ever imagined.

Leaders and aspiring leaders who have developed portfolios acknowledge that it is a time and labor-intensive process. Most say that once the structure has been determined and the artifacts selected, the rest of the portfolio can be completed in approximately 8 to 10 hours. The consensus is that it is well worth the time and effort.

How can all that is required in the career advancement portfolio be included without making it too lengthy?

Creators of career advancement portfolios admit to initially wanting to include all the artifacts they have collected and to write extremely comprehensive reflections to make sure that reviewers are convinced that they have the experiences and skills to perform successfully in the position. It is absolutely critical that, should you share this urge, you control it!

Our research reveals that potential employers will not review materials that are too lengthy. Your goal is for your materials to be noticed and thoroughly reviewed. You also want to portray your consideration of others' time. One or two carefully selected artifacts and a succinct and well-written reflection (no more than two or three paragraphs; one page maximum) for each leadership criteria or job function is ample. Although you must include all five steps of the reflection cycle, you need write only one to three well-worded sentences on each step. Remember that reviewers have other opportunities to learn about you. Your leadership framework, letter of application, and résumé all offer valuable insights into your style, skills, experiences, and capabilities.

Which portfolio is the most effective—electronic or hard copy?

Each form of the portfolio has advantages, depending on the situation. Because the content of each is the same, many applicants are creating both. Transferring a hard copy portfolio to electronic medium is relatively easy. Of course, you may need to add multimedia. There is no doubt that the electronic career advancement portfolio demonstrates your technological expertise. Many are finding it advantageous to send a letter of e-mail thanks to the interviewer for selecting him or her for an interview, and at that time they place the URL web address in the e-mail for the interviewer to link to in order to review his or her portfolio. Some applicants present the paper portfolio at the interview and then leave a disk or CD-ROM for interviewers to view at their convenience.

Others who are really comfortable with technology are able to set up computer equipment in the interview room ahead of time and present their PowerPoint® portfolios during the interview. Several applicants have said, however, that having to concentrate on the technology during the interview would distract them or make them nervous. Using the paper portfolio during the interview session would be best if this is the case, as you would not want anything to interfere with your ability to be confident and poised during the interview.

RESOURCE

Sample Career Advancement Portfolio

Career Advancement Portfolio
of
Sue Jones

Table of Contents

Introduction

Résumé

Leadership Framework

Professional Goals

Artifacts and Reflections of Leadership Domains

- Learner-Centered Leadership
- Learner-Centered Climate
- Learner-Centered Curriculum and Instruction
- Learner-Centered Professional Development
- Equity in Excellence for All Learners
- Learner-Centered Communication
- Planning and Management of Resources to Support the Learning Environment

Introduction

I have developed my career advancement portfolio so that you can better assess my skills as a leader. You will find my most recent résumé. You will also find my leadership framework that will provide you with my philosophy of education and leadership. I have also included my 5-year professional goals and artifacts and reflections of my past year's involvement as a leader on my campus. The reflections allow you to get an inside view of some of my most recent educational experiences, as well as how I will use those experiences to further my leadership capabilities.

Résumé

SUE JONES
111 N. E Street
Huntsville, TX 77777
409-294-1000

CAREER OBJECTIVE: To obtain an elementary principal's position in the Post School District

EDUCATION:
M.Ed. Administration
Sam Houston State University, Huntsville, TX
B.A. Education/Psychology
Yale University, New Haven, CT

CERTIFICATION:
Texas Mid-Management Certificate, Assistant Principal (PK-12), Life
Texas Elementary Certificate (Grades 1-8), Life
Massachusetts Elementary Certificate (Grades K-8), Life
Rhode Island Provisional Elementary Certificate (7 Year Expired)
Connecticut Provisional Elementary Certificate (5 Year Expired)

EDUCATIONAL EXPERIENCE:

1990–Present	GREENWAY ELEMENTARY SCHOOL Cook School District Instructional Technology Coordinator	The Woodlands, TX
1990–Present	BAYLOR COLLEGE OF MEDICINE Summer Science, Technology, and Math Institute Instructor	Houston, TX
1984–1985	MARGARET NEARY SCHOOL Algonquin Regional School District Grade 6 Computer Resource/LOGO Teacher	Southboro, MA
1984	UNIVERSITY OF MASSACHUSETTS Computer Sports Camp BASIC Teacher/Consultant	Amherst, MA
1974–1974	CENTRAL SCHOOL Pentucket Regional School System Grade 2 Classroom Teacher	West Newbury, MA
1969–1971	ADA S. HAWKINS SCHOOL Foster-Glocester Regional School System Grade 3 Classroom Teacher	Harmony, RI
1968–1969	A.W. COX SCHOOL Guilford School System Grade 2 Classroom Teacher	Guilford, CT

AFFILIATIONS & HONORS:
CISD "Second Mile Award" Recipient, 1998
Greenway Elementary CISD "Humanitarian" Award, 1996
Texas Computer Educators' Association (TCEA)
Texas Association of Educational Technology (TAET)
Delta Kappa Gamma

COMPETENCIES:	*Interview Skills*
	Sam Houston State University Interview Committee, 1999
	Financial Skills
	Technology Fundraiser Chairperson, 1998
	Collaboration Skills
	Team Leader
	Grant-Writing Skills
	Technology Chairperson/Grant Writer
	CHAMPS Peer Tutoring Chairperson
	Staff Development Skills
	Technology Workshop Presenter

Campus/District Committees:

1991-Present

Decision Making

Budget

Policy

Social

Sci-Tech

Technology Fair

CISD Total Quality Management Team

CBAM Team

School Team Training

Computer Curriculum Committee

District Technology Planning Committee

Site-Based Decision-Making Committee

Educational Improvement Council

PROFESSIONAL DEVELOPMENT:

TAAS Alignment and Strategies, 1998

Instructional Leadership Training, 1998

TEKS Alignment for Technology, 1998

Project Learning Tree (CISD), 1997–1998

Gifted/Talented Certification, 1997

TCEA State Conventions 1990–Present
(Presenter of "Integrating Technology with Elementary Hands-On Science & Math," 1997 State Conference)

TCEA ESC Region 6, Area IV Conferences, 1990–Present
(Steering Committee and Presenter of "PowerPoint" and "Web Page Construction," 1997)

Metropolitan Association for Teachers of Science Conference, 1995

District Workshop Presenter (Inspiration, MS Office, Curricular Programs, E-mail, TENET, Internet, World Wide Web, Excelsior Grade 2)

District Workshops (Access, Network, Connectivity, Netscape and Netscape Mail, Web Page Construction, Video Conferencing, Peer Coaching, Excelsior Grade 2, TQM, Conflict Resolution, Developing Capable People)

National Educators' Computer Convention (NECC), 1992, 1994

Reference Register

Data-Driven Decision Making
Ms. Lisa Gail, Principal
Shady Pines Elementary
203 Shady Pine Road
Southboro, MA 93082
409-555-5555, e-mail: lgail@dhdu.edu

Community Partnerships
Mr. Kyle Overcon, Chair of Campus Improvement Team
Ballard High School
345 High Horse Lane
Houston, Texas 75777
903-845-3343, e-mail: kxo@shsu.edu

Organizational Management
Dr. Jennifer Smith, Superintendent
Rollingbrook School District
4567 West Creek Road
The Woodlands, Texas 77388
281-396-0464, e-mail: jsmith@shsu.edu

Curriculum/Instruction/Assessment
Mr. Mac Gilliam, Assistant Principal
7890 Check Boulevard
The Woodlands, Texas 77341
409-291-3247, email: mgfair@shsu.edu

Professional Development
Dr. Jerald Lowehauser, Assistant Superintendent of Curriculum
Cook School District
4567 Jumping Fish Trail
The Woodlands, Texas 77356
409-348-2910, e-mail: fstory@tsds.edu

Leadership Framework

Leadership Framework
Sue Jones

Philosophy of Education

The purpose of education is to provide an arena for all to become lifelong learners. When individuals are motivated by sufficient opportunities in a supportive environment, they can become positive, productive, contributing members of society. Education's focus should be that of ensuring that those opportunities are made available to all.

Philosophy of Leadership

An effective participatory leader needs to be credible and have a vision that guides him or her toward specific goals. That vision needs to be shared in order to receive support before it can be initiated. Leaders need to be committed to motivating and empowering teachers and students toward a common goal. Leadership is a process of influencing others to attain a mutual goal for a group.

Vision for Learners

Children learn best when their individual learning styles are addressed. A principal needs to provide a safe, supportive environment, which encourages each child to reach his or her fullest potential. A principal should believe, and ensure that his or her staff believes, that all children have the ability to learn.

Vision for Teachers

Teachers hold the future in their hands. An atmosphere of trust and respect in which individuals feel valued needs to be established in their workplace. It is the principal's responsibility to foster such a climate through a positive attitude, supportive collaboration, and open communication that allows for input and feedback. If teachers are made to feel like they are valuable resources, they then are in a position to make learning a positive experience for children.

Vision for the Organization

The leader should provide a positive environment where all can learn through an empowered teaching staff and collaborative efforts with the community. Building and fostering relationships with parent organizations and volunteers as well as establishing partnerships with area businesses are a necessary part of the foundation. An environment of mutual respect for individual differences as well as pride in the school and in the educational learning process also needs to be evident.

Professional Growth

Professional development for educators should be a continual process if teachers are to be considered lifelong learners. Adequate resources need to be acquired to provide teachers and staff with training and inservices to keep up with current trends, such as mentoring. Because training should be relevant to the instructional process, the staff should be surveyed to determine their professional needs. Constructive feedback is one method of assessment that could be used to determine if growth has occurred.

Method of Vision Attainment

A principal must try to encourage everyone to embrace his or her vision by sharing it with staff, community members, and students. The principal needs to show all stakeholders that he or she is committed to providing the best education possible. This can be accomplished with respect, support, empathy, encouragement, organization, responsibility, visibility, observation, positive actions, and listening. The principal needs to "walk the walk," not just "talk the talk." He or she needs to demonstrate ownership of the school through his or her actions.

Professional Goals

FIVE-YEAR
PROFESSIONAL GOALS

1. Establish and maintain a school climate conducive to learning for both students and teachers

2. Think proactively to avert responding to situations in a reactive manner

3. Continue the integration of technology relevant to the curriculum

4. Provide needs-based staff development for the campus

5. Establish and maintain open lines of communication between administration, staff, and the community

Artifacts and Reflections
of
Leadership Domains

Campus Improvement Plan

Task	Timeline	Person Responsible
Area: technology integration 1. Form a committee to investigate ways to provide more current hardware and software as well as methods to continue integration with the curriculum (consider sources of funding—PTO, fund-raiser, reorganization of campus budget, etc.).	September 1998–February 1999	Technology coordinator

Learner-Centered Leadership

One of the goals of Greenway Elementary's Campus Improvement Plan for the 1998-1999 year dealt with technology. Studying ways to provide more current hardware and software as well as methods to continue integration with the curriculum were the objectives. As the instructional technology coordinator of the campus, I formed a committee consisting of teachers representing all grade levels. Our major charge was to find a way to either upgrade or purchase new computers with a Windows 98 operating system.

In the past, the PTO had been able to provide some funding for our technological efforts, but because we wanted to re-outfit the lab with 26 computers, we felt we needed to come up with a plan that wouldn't rely so heavily on their generosity or deplete their entire year's budget. The committee decided on a fundraiser, which would be a collaborative effort involving the entire campus: students, teachers, administrators, and parents. Ultimately, responsibility for the event rested with the committee and the teachers, but the PTO members' team spirit, time, and energy were gratefully accepted.

Even though participation by classes, teachers, and the PTO was voluntary, it turned out that there was 100% involvement by the learning community. The feeling of camaraderie and being a part of something that would benefit everyone, along with the enthusiasm that was generated, all contributed to the evening's success. The $12,000 profit enabled our school to realize one of its goals to provide our students with the equipment necessary to take advantage of the resources technology has to offer education.

Attempting to involve the entire campus in a collaborative effort was a huge undertaking, but the rewards of realizing a goal, being supported by the entire learning community, and sensing everyone's enthusiastic involvement in the innovative event were well worth the risk taken. As a principal, I would use this collaborative or inquiring group approach to accomplish such a task.

INVITATION!!!!

It's back to school time and you are invited to Del Lago for the weekend —all expenses paid!!

We are having a retreat for our campus teachers and the district administrators. The retreat begins Friday night at 6:00 with a fish fry. Saturday we will begin our sessions at 8:00 with a Mariachi breakfast. We will be in work sessions during the day and end our retreat by 6:00 p.m., Saturday evening.

We are so excited about this great opportunity to work together and welcome our new faculty members. See you at Del Lago!!!

Learner-Centered Climate

Because resistance to change is often evident, an administrator needs to anticipate its possible presence and try to deal with it in a proactive manner. A few years ago, my campus was not only faced with a new administration for the third time in 4 years, but the position was filled by a first-year principal from outside the district who had to deal with a staff consisting mostly of veteran teachers. Our school was also beginning its first year as a pilot site for technology integration, which meant that the teachers needed to be trained in using technology.

In an attempt to ease the transition, the teachers and district-level administrators were first invited to attend a team-building weekend at a nearby resort. Then, when school began, another teacher and I were asked to join a Total Quality Management (TQM) team consisting of the new principal and district level administrators, which included the director of staff development, director of curriculum, personnel director, and assistant superintendent (our former principal of one year). In addition, I became a member of the Concerns Based Adoption Model (CBAM) team along with some other teachers from my school to help deal with concerns.

The team-based activities, the TQM training, and the CBAM project all seemed to be proactive methods of dealing with change in a positive manner. They introduced the staff to paradigm shifts and tried to give those involved a sense of empowerment. These tools encouraged an atmosphere of creativity, innovation, and mutual respect exemplified in a supportive, trusting environment.

As an administrator, I think it is important to be able to recognize that certain barriers might prevent establishing the type of productive, open atmosphere one had hoped for in an effective learning environment. Serving on the above committees has given me some insight and broadened my understanding of the importance of cultivating a positive climate.

Memorandum

TO: First-Grade Teaching Team

FROM: Sue Jones
                Technology Coordinator

RE: New Software

DATE: November 1, 1999

Please be aware that the new software packages you requested have arrived. Those packages are: Inspirations, Math for the Real World, and Excel. On November 4, 1999, from 3:30–4:30, we will have a workshop about the use of Inspirations. Ms. Smith, the first-grade Team Leader, will conduct this workshop. On that day, she and I will coordinate other dates and times for inservice to address the other two computer programs. We look forward to your attendance at the November 4th workshop and to your implementation of the new software into your curriculum.

Learner-Centered Curriculum and Instruction

One of the district goals is "to provide all teachers, students, and staff with the tools, skills, and support to effectively enhance learning and decision making." One of our campus objectives is to explore and use computer software to develop higher-order thinking skills. In my role as instructional technologist at my campus, I was responsible for recommending software that would integrate technology into the curriculum, providing training to teachers, and reporting the progress to the budget and site-based committees as well as to the district technology directors. The selection and rationalization for use of, and consequent effectiveness of, the problem-solving software were directly related to the implementation of the best practices in curriculum and instruction.

The programs that our campus used to promote higher-order thinking skills included "Inspiration," for mind mapping; "Math for the Real World," for motivating and challenging students to apply their mathematical skills; and "Excel," for drawing conclusions and making generalizations from data. Each one of these software packages was chosen for its correlation to curricular integration.

Teachers and students of all levels were able to use Inspiration to brainstorm ideas, connect their words, and establish relationships while constructing diagrams and outlines of their thoughts. The enthusiasm that students, teachers, and parents exhibited for the Math for the Real World program was contagious; even students who had previously disliked math were excited about seeking solutions to the mathematical problems the program generated. Entering information into an Excel spreadsheet and then charting it for data analysis provided yet another medium for students to increase their critical-thinking ability. All of the programs corresponded with TAAS and TEKS objectives.

My involvement in the effective integration of technology into the curriculum has affected two of my goals as a future administrator: to continue seeking ways to link technology to curricular and instructional strategies and to provide staff development that will help attain achievement of those needs. Administratively, I would engage the support of the teachers through committees to plan collaboratively in securing tools that provide relevance to successful learning.

INSERVICE DAY

August 5, 2000

Computer Lab

Title:	Computerized Gradebook
Time:	8:15–10:45 a.m.
Presenters:	Sue Jones, Sarah Smith, and Jackie Goodson

Coffee and donuts served from 7:30–8:15

Learner-Centered Professional Development

Yearly computer education conferences held at the local, regional, state, and national levels have provided a means for interested individuals to be a part of the planning, attending, and/or presenting. In the past 9 years, I have been able to take advantage of many opportunities and bring the knowledge back to my campus and district. I have done this by serving on curriculum committees for technology integration and providing inservices and minisessions. Technological advances occur at such a rapid rate that it is imperative for someone in the field to stay current. For that reason, I see my involvement as an essential element to both others' technological education and mine.

One of the strongest avenues through which continuous learning improves is having the ability to not only acquire knowledge but to also be able to share it with others. One such opportunity for learning was provided by my district when I was sent (and was able to bring along two classroom teachers from my school) to Colorado to learn how to use a specific gradebook program that the district was considering purchasing.

During an inservice day that was conducted before the opening of school, the two teachers and I presented a customized hands-on session. The session provided information that enabled each teacher to enter his or her class roster, individualize it to his or her situation, and walk away with a computerized gradebook ready for the first assignment to be entered. The information that the trained classroom teachers were able to give, the customization of the gradebook for our faculty's use, and the positive manner in which the workshop was presented were all contributing factors to the workshop's success and each individual's professional growth. Since then I have been asked to share the knowledge that I gained about the gradebook program with other schools in our district.

Each time I present a workshop, it is a learning experience for me. Presenting offers me an avenue for self-evaluation and an opportunity to connect with my audience. I gain confidence if the session is well received, and it provides feedback for improving methods when necessary.

Knowing that the key to introducing, synthesizing, and using new information lies in the ability to get others on board with you is essential to the success of reform and innovation. It is personally gratifying for me to observe that my involvement with professional development has led to the professional growth of others; we have both accomplished a win-win situation.

BEFORE-SCHOOL TUTORING

If you would like for your child to receive before-school assistance with reading, math, or writing, please contact your child's teacher at 499-999-9999 or return the attached form.

What is provided?

Breakfast snacks

Transportation

How long will my child be at school before hours?

30 minutes

*Please contact your child's teacher or return the attached form if you wish for your child to participate.

Equity in Excellence for All Learners

Although my campus serves a population that is primarily white, English speaking, and socioeconomically secure, there is some diversification in the learning levels of students. The special education department collaborates with the classroom teachers in modifying the curriculum, providing content mastery, and coteaching to address special needs. To ensure that all children are afforded the chance to succeed, tutoring sessions are established for any student who exhibits weakness in a core subject area.

The teachers or parent volunteers offer some tutoring throughout the year on a one-to-one basis, but the most extensive tutoring sessions are those that occur when weaknesses are diagnosed prior to TAAS testing. If a deficiency in scores is noted with regard to a particular ethnicity, gender, or language, the situation receives attention. In addition, every student who has been diagnosed as needing remediation or reteaching is targeted and given the opportunity to receive extra help. Letters are then sent out to the parents of these students explaining the opportunity offered by the school. This effort is a collaborative one shared by the campuswide professional teaching community whose goal is to level the playing field of standardized testing for the entire student population.

The tutoring sessions are held for 30 to 40 minutes before the beginning of the school day, involve small group instruction, and offer incentives for attendance and extra work completed at home. Any child predicted to be at risk for failing the state-mandated testing is encouraged to participate. In this way, each student is provided the opportunity to achieve passing state-imposed standards.

I believe the method of ascertaining the proficiencies necessary to pass a standardized test is valid. It has the capability of responding to the needs of many individual learners with different learning capabilities.

As a future administrator, I would find it advantageous to determine the school's culture in order to promote an environment conducive to all learners. An effective administrator needs to be aware of any diversity that could affect his or her learning community. The diversity (or nondiversity) that exists must be addressed.

Press Release

To be released immediately to the *Daily Times*

TechNovember Nites

The Greenway Elementary campus teachers will be conducting training sessions for the community on Microsoft Office computer programs during the month of November for 2 hours each night. The schedule of presentations is as follows:

November 7, 1998   6:00–8:00 p.m.   Computer Lab   Microsoft Word

November 14, 1998   6:00–8:00 p.m.   Computer Lab   PowerPoint

November 21, 1998   6:00–8:00 p.m.   Computer Lab   Excel

We can accommodate up to 30 individuals in each session. Please contact Joan Reed at 488-999-9999 to enroll in these upcoming sessions.

Learner-Centered Communication

The relationship between a school and the community it serves needs to be positive for the two to effectively coexist. I believe that promoting good relations is a valuable key that helps to ensure the best for our students. With that in mind, a plan was developed to give something back to the adults in the district—free computer classes. Technology has become an integral part of almost everyone's life, yet there are some people who have not had the opportunity to explore its possibilities.

A series of introductory evening computer classes was offered at my school based on the realization that many community members might be interested in becoming, or need to become, computer literate. The first step was to advertise, so an article was placed in the local newspapers describing "TechNovember Nites" and explaining how to reserve a place to learn the following Microsoft Office programs: MS Word, PowerPoint, and Excel.

The response was overwhelming—adults of all ages attended. The experience would have been gratifying if only one community member's educational needs had been met, but it was even more so because the effort helped so many. The classes were repeated in the spring when parent volunteers were given the opportunity to attend the classes during the school day.

I believe that this venture proved to be incredibly worthwhile and I would consider offering it again to positively connect with the community that my campus serves. It would be a way of communicating to the school community that education can be a process of lifelong learning and that our school cares about promoting that ethic.

Schedule for Keyboarding

Submitted to

All Greenway Elementary Teachers
For review and revision

By
Sue Jones
Technology Coordinator

September 20, 1998

*Please check the attached schedule, make any revisions, and place the revised schedule in my box by September 25, 1998.

Planning and Management of Resources to Support the Learning Environment

The support staff at our school has been responsible for performing various duties including clerical tasks, operating the copy machines, discipline management, monitoring the cafeteria, bus duty assignments, and graphic design projects. This year, due to safety factors, it became necessary to reduce the size of the physical education classes. A plan was then devised which would not only alleviate the number problem but would also provide an opportunity for each student to learn keyboarding techniques referred to in the technology applications of the TEKS.

The physical education teacher and I collaborated in establishing a rotating schedule of classes, which involved each class attending keyboarding once a week, excluding Friday. Two of the support staff were trained as instructional aides who would each monitor the keyboarding progress of their chosen grade level for half a day while remaining available for other miscellaneous duties such as troubleshooting technological problems and graphic design. On Friday, each aide assisted the physical education classes. I was responsible for monitoring and evaluating the aides, charting each student's quarterly progress, assigning a grade for the course, and distributing the grades to the classroom teacher.

The success of the plan is twofold: a keyboarding program was established that provided a means to meet state requirements for technology and a safer environment for learning was furnished to the physical education classes. The recognition and maximization of the talents of our campus support personnel and the collaborative effort of the teachers, physical education department, and administration accomplished both endeavors.

Involvement in the establishment of the keyboarding program and its success has been rewarding for me as a professional. It has made me realize the importance of the role played by the management of valuable resources in supporting a more effective and safer learning environment. Students had a chance to relate the use of technology to their daily learning through keyboarding while teachers and parents were pleased with how the resulting proficiency benefited their child's educational process.

CORWIN
PRESS

The Corwin Press logo—a raven striding across an open book—represents the happy union of courage andlearning. We area professional-level publisher of books and journals for K-12 educators, and we are committed to creating and providing resources that embody these qualities. Corwin's motto is "Success for All Learners."